FORGING NATIONS:

A Comparative View

of Rural Ferment and Revolt

EDITED BY

JOSEPH SPIELBERG

SCOTT WHITEFORD

MICHIGAN STATE UNIVERSITY PRESS

1976

Contents

Preface

THE PAPERS THAT CONSTITUTE THIS BOOK WERE FIRST PRESENTED IN A symposium on comparative peasant movements, held at Michigan State University in May 1974. The symposium format included a formal presentation after each paper by a discussant who had extensive knowledge about the region analyzed in the paper. This, in turn, was followed by an open discussion period. Because of limitations on the length of this volume, we did not include the discussion but have attempted to raise some of the major points of the discussants in the Introduction.

The following members of the Michigan State University faculty were discussants of individual papers and contributed to the success of the symposium: Drs. David Bailey, Stanley Chojnacki, Arthur Rubel, Charles Morrison, and John Henderson.

We would like to thank Dr. Bernard Gallin, Chairman of the Department of Anthropology, who chaired the symposium; Dr. Stanley Brandes, Dr. Bill Derman, and Ms. Tracy Kowalski for helping organize the symposium. The symposium received generous support from the following departments, centers, and institute: Agricultural Economics, Anthropology, Geography, History, Sociology, African Studies Center, Asian Studies Center, Latin American Studies Center, International Studies and Programs, and the Institute of Comparative Sociology. The publication of this volume was made possible through a grant provided by the College of Social Science.

Introduction

JOSEPH SPIELBERG

and

SCOTT WHITEFORD

RURAL POPULATIONS, DESPITE ETHNIC, RELIGIOUS, AND ECONOMIC heterogeneity, often provide the raw material from which nations passing through armed confrontation are initially forged and cast. Despite their inexorable incorporation into new or old national economic and political structure, they almost always find themselves at the bottom and their hold on the "home" terrain weakened. They give their surpluses, if not more, and receive little in return. Only the uninformed could assume that the rural denizens are happy or at the very least indifferent to the price they must pay for the "privilege" of citizenship. The struggles of rural people to gain greater power and control within their national structures, or to free themselves from the inequities entirely, have created and continue to create violent or contentious currents in the contemporary world. A countryside in the state of ferment and on the threshold of rebellion is the sine qua non (or symptom) of a nation struggling to be born or of one born deformed.

It is hoped that this volume will contribute to our understanding of the forces creating the ferment and struggle of the peasant within the process of building or tempering a nation. The chapters examine collective rural mobilization in different regions of the world: Europe, Tanzania, Mozambique, Mexico, Bengal, and South Texas. The authors of the papers, representing various academic disciplines, were asked to address the following questions:

1. What forms of organization, if any, have developed or are in the process of developing among the peasantry in order to gain access to or elicit a response from the nation-state level of decision-making and resource allocation?

2. What factors (historical, sociocultural, or geographical) have facilitated or hindered the sociopolitical mobilization and its particular forms of organization in these distinct areas?

3. What, specifically, have been the formal and informal means of articulation between urban-based segments of the society (labor, students, intellectuals, etc.) and the rural sectors in the development, or the lack of it, of peasant political organization?

From a comparative standpoint, the answers to these questions imply certain interrelated universal dimensions or processes that emerge in all of the articles. These are:

(1) the spread and enforcement of compulsory, governmental institutions, i.e., statemaking;

(2) the establishment and maintenance of internal regimentation for political action within the rural population; and

(3) the growth and spread of capitalism and the subsequent proletarianization of rural producers.

With increased technological efficiency, history has been marked by centralization of power within territorial units leading to the growth of states. With this has come the spread and enforcement of participation in compulsory government institutions or programs such as military conscription, taxation, and education. The locus of power and governmental site of these institutionalized programs has been the city. Although rural people are often only a resource in the struggle for power, it should not be assumed that they have been passive in this process. Rural unrest and mobilization are often predicated on the desire of rural dwellers either to curb the centralized power impinging on their lives or to gain greater input and influence with respect to the goals and procedures of their government's institutional tentacles. Nevertheless, the nature and extent of these intrusions will influence the developmental history of rural resistance and mobilization.

The creation of organizations within the rural population— whether these be peasant unions, political parties, or guerrilla bands

2

—is imperative if the people are to achieve greater control of or influence on the increasingly centralized decision-making and re-source-allocation structures of the nation-state. Furthermore, whether the immediate objectives of such organizations be the winning of an election, the demonstration of protest or dissatisfaction, or the paramilitary "liberation" of a given territorial or institutional unit, neither the organizations nor the immediate objective can be obtained without a certain degree of effective regimentation. More specifically, mobilization itself will require the development of lines of communication, a division of labor, a focus of authority, an apparatus for recruitment, and, on a more ideological level, the establishment of a supportive rationale based on a supposed commonality of interest, i.e., class consciousness.

Such mobilization and its prerequisites for regimentation are not always easy to attain. In short, the ability to develop and maintain such organization is hindered by internal, traditional antagonisms based on cultural, class, or ideological differences; limited sustaining material resources and organizational expertise; and the degree of dependency on internal or international resources, especially as these affect the propensity to take risks. On a microlevel, dependency is often manifested in a series of very specific intersocietal linkages, such as patron-client relationships. In many cases the eventual success or failure achieved in mobilization depends, very critically, on the possibility of creating alternatives to such linkages.

No examination of particular rural movements in the world today would be complete without considering the growth and spread of capitalism. This historical process permeates both ends of the structural spectrum or nexus just outlined. On the one hand, it is often the sought-after type of social formation (with its attendant cultural dimensions) that both spurs the development of centralized power and determines its forms of rural penetration. On the other hand, it leads to the proletarianization of peasant populations, thereby creating a principal source of unrest and the object of rural sociopolitical mobilization and organization.

Charles Tilly's chapter, "Rural Collective Action in Modern Europe," represents an outstanding and provocative effort both for the student of peasant movements in Europe, as well as for those with a more general interest in the topic. While this chapter offers us, primarily, a comprehensive configuration of peasant movements in Europe since 1500, it also serves us a model of great potential for clarifying the numerous complex, but specific, issues that such a topic must deal with in any setting. His configuration places rural collective action or movements in the context of macroscopic, long-range processes now acknowledged as being worldwide forces: namely, the development of centralized modern states, urbanization, and capitalism. Simultaneously, his configuration discriminates between distinctive types of rural collective action, characteristic of distinct historical periods, and relates these to the particular patterns of interrelations that obtained between states, urbanization, and capitalism.

Not only is Tilly's contribution rich in insight and fresh in perspective, it is also provocative in compelling us to evaluate conceptual alternatives with respect to major issues. Tilly's analysis forces us to carefully examine the possibility of significant qualitative differences between the early modern state and the traditional judicial and political power groups of the seignorial regime. His contribution makes us consider the relative conceptual weight one is to place on continuity versus evolution of forms of protest or collective action. Finally, and perhaps most significantly, Professor Tilly forces us to consider two significantly different interpretations of the fundamental nature of rural collective action. Namely, do peasants organize collectively to resist forces that are challenging their traditional existence or because they have been denied access to improvements in their condition?

John Broomfield examines the failure of repeated efforts to mobilize the peasants of Bengal during the twentieth century. Broomfield points out the danger of looking at rural mobilization as separated from urban populations because of the overlapping networks and processes that tie individuals in the different localities together. His analysis points to the importance of a comparative concern with regional elites and their varying degrees and sources of power, and types of association with the peasantry. Perhaps the most intriguing aspect of the chapter on Bengal is Broomfield's lucid discussion of how emic categories, such as landlord, moneylender, and peasant, which both colonial rulers and urban organizers have used to order social structure in rural Bengal, are not discrete roles. A single person may be each with different people, establishing a network of ties in which he has many patrons as well as many clients—depending on the situational context, identity, and interest change. As Broomfield points out "fat cats and thin [there are], but they are not ranked and neatly ordered" into neat legal or emic categories. Patron-client relationships emerge as a salient structure working with caste and religious divisions to keep rural workers or peasants horizontally factionalized and difficult to mobilize.

The uniqueness of the Mexican Revolution, in Professor Katz's treatment, resolves itself into a paradox. While the Mexican Revolution was a most profound social upheaval, essentially agrarian in nature and involving the participation of peasants or peasantlike people, primarily, no large-scale redistribution of lands took place until 1934, twenty-four years after its eruption.

In seeking answers or resolutions to this paradox, Katz highlights both internal and external factors. Internally, he describes the diversity and differential distribution of various peasantlike populations between southern and northern Mexico. This factor, coupled with the corresponding differences in the class origins and ideological orientations of southern versus northern revolutionary leaders and the degree of national prominence and national popular support achieved by the latter, effectively blunted, if only for a time, the process of or the genuine commitment to effective land redistribution. More importantly, however, in Katz's model was the external factor: the proximity and influence of American corporate and political interests among the revolutionary leaders of the northern movement.

John Saul, like the other authors in this book, examines the groups that mediate between peasants and the larger society; but, in contrast to the others, Saul is particularly concerned with the peasants' potential as a socialist revolutionary force that can bring about the "transformation of the status quo of colonialism and neo-colonialism." Saul's first task is to establish the existence of a peasantry in Africa. His definition of peasantry incorporates a range of rural dwellers whose variation he points to as an important factor explaining revolutionary potential. He proceeds to examine the forces that created the African peasantry, concluding that imperialism has been the dominant force in the making of the African peasant. Capitalism, Saul suggests, both creates and destroys the peasantry. The chapter then discusses the development of shared consciousness and the potential for political action against those who control the salient resources. Saul is especially concerned with the type of organization that can most effectively incorporate peasant participation in the revolutionary process. The empirical cases analyzed are Mozambique and Tanzania; in both instances a conscious effort has been made to draw the peasants into revolutionary activity and to maintain their participation.

To the students of the contemporary American scene, civil rights agitation and activity among Chicanos tend to evoke more an image of agrarian radicalism and outright rural revolt than any other type of movement today. Such an image might simply be a matter of conjuring up visions of striking grape pickers in California or an armed raid on a remote New Mexico county courthouse. John Shockley's paper, however, demonstrates that such an image may have more substance than just a casual association of an ethnic group with one or two dramatic events. More specifically, Shockley examines the growth of an independent Chicano political movement and the extent to which landless, migratory agricultural laborers have been an important force within the specific development and stages of this movement. Using both his background as a political scientist and the borrowed skills of an anthropologist, Shockley analyzes electoral returns and the expressed opinions of participants in Crystal City and Zavala County, Texas. Based on his analysis he demonstrates how different patterns in types of intersocietal linkages played a decisive role in reversing a long-standing pattern of ethnic, class political and social domination. In addition, he examines the potential such patterned linkages may have in limiting or accelerating the spread of such a political movement or revolt among the Chicanos of South Texas.

On a higher level of analytical complexity, his paper also gives considerable attention to new organizational frameworks and styles of indigenous leadership, as these articulate with the particular patterns in local level relationships to property, labor, and communication links. Shockley's contribution, in our opinion, is a daring one; daring in that it takes a relatively unorthodox approach to a contemporary American phenomenon usually conceived in different terms; daring also in that it examines a phenomenon that is fast-breaking and ongoing, and therefore one that offers many hazards to those who venture to predict its course and ultimate outcome.

Richard N. Adams was asked by the organizers of the conference to compare the points and issues raised in the papers. This he developed and refined for the final chapter of this volume. Adams uses a comparative evolutionary framework, in which he examines the studies presented in the previous chapters, to disentangle the interplay between capitalism and the growth and concentration of state power. The result is a penetrating and provocative chapter. Adams suggests that the state is the source of the salient variables that generate and terminate rural collective movements. Capitalism is shown to be a constellation of devices used by statemakers. With the development of capitalism the market became an arena in which one society could gain at the expense of another. Thus, capitalism was used by states to increase their power. With increased power, societies added levels of integration, and the peasant became increasingly subordinated. Adams proceeds to differentiate between rural movements that develop in an effort to curb the usurpation of power "that capitalism provides for the capitalist and the state," and between rural movements that develop as an effort to gain access to the power of the state. Regardless of efforts at mobilization, however, Adams concludes that history and evolution have made an anachronism of the peasant. The passing of kingdoms has left them with no enduring anchoring point in the larger social order. The nation-state, whether socialist or capitalist, it would seem, will accept them as citizens and/or commodities, but not as peasants.

The nature of rural movements is obviously a broad theme. Peasants, rural proletarians, village artisans, and traders are integral parts of rural society in most areas of the world; the interaction of these separate groups becomes inevitable and indispensable when rural mobilization occurs. Rural movements merit study because they often represent the setting in which different groups organize,

7

articulate, and attempt to change or maintain their way of life against changing socioeconomic structures. Looked at in this fashion, rural movements can be considered to contain the principal processes of nation-making.

But the issues discussed in this volume are in a real sense not merely "academic." Unequal distribution and control of resources is characteristic of most nations of the world. The disenfranchised populations throughout the world, predominately rural, will continue to demand their rightful place and greater participation in the national political process and economic structures. The forces creating and in some cases restricting this struggle, and their repercussions are the central concern of this volume.

Rural Collective Action in Modern Europe

CHARLES TILLY

EUROPE'S PEASANTS PAID FOR THE EXPANSION OF CAPITALISM.
They also paid for the rise of national states. Peasants paid directly
by producing or yielding the bulk of the requisite land, labor, commodities, and capital. And they paid indirectly by losing their collective control over the local disposition of these very same factors. In
the process, they stopped being peasants. They often fought both
against the demands that they pay and against the threats to their
peasanthood. In the short run, they sometimes won. In the long run,
however, they lost.

By today peasants have almost disappeared from the European
landscape. As peasants they have lost almost all their power. Their
successors, the rural proletarians and commercial farmers, have
fought on both sides: against the increasing pressure of the state and
the market, and for a share of control over the state and the market.
On the whole, Europe's rural populations have been less intensely
involved in large-scale struggles for power than have the people of
cities. Yet their involvement has not been negligible. At a local scale,
the rural population has often been intensely involved in struggles for
power. This essay surveys the forms and loci of that involvement
over the last few hundred years.

In order to get a good look at that changing involvement, we must
cut ourselves a somewhat bigger peephole; to put peasant action in
context, the discussion will treat the rural population as a whole, and
make comparisons within it. With so broad a subject, the analysis
will be incomplete and the evidence fragmentary. If we can arrive at
a plausible general statement of the conditions for peasant action in
modern Europe and develop a preliminary sense of the differences

between the peasantry and the rest of the rural population, that will have to suffice.

This paper is partly descriptive and partly analytical. On the descriptive side, it enumerates some of the broad structural changes in the European countryside over the past few centuries, some of the chief means by which rural Europeans have carried on collective action, and some of the main ways in which the predominant forms of collective action have changed. On the analytic side, it suggests some explanations for the changes and variations in predominant forms of collective action. The explanations have to do mainly with the growth of capitalism, the expansion of national states, and the consequent transformation of rural social structure. Then, only then, come comments on the conditions under which sustained peasant movements arise and on the conditions in which they achieve their objectives.

What Sort of Peasant?

Let us take peasants to be members of households whose major activity is farming, households that produce a major part of the goods and services they consume, that exercise substantial control over the land they farm, and that supply the major part of their labor requirements from their own energies. If we then take "rural" to mean those areas in which agriculture is the predominant activity, Europe's rural population has long included a wide variety of people besides peasants. In the rural comedy, the woodchopper, the carter, the nun, the smith are stock figures. Within agriculture itself, the landlord, the cash-crop specialist, the hired hand, the day-laborer, the servant, the migratory harvest worker, the part-time artisan have all played crucial parts both in production and in politics. Each major class of the rural population has had a characteristically different form of involvement in conflict.

Nevertheless, until recent times Europe was one of the world's major areas of peasant agriculture. Until recently the majority of the European population consisted of peasants. We can therefore reasonably concentrate on the actions of peasants while trying to distinguish peasants from the rest of the rural population, and while trying to relate the peasants to the nonpeasants.

10

The real European peasants little resembled their conventional portraits. Demographic historians are beginning to reveal a European peasantry that was fairly mobile on the small geographic scale, that controlled its fertility in a crudely rational way, that responded sensitively to changes in the prices of commodities and of labor. We discover an active market in rural land and a well-developed flow of agricultural products to cities long before the nineteenth century. We discover—as we shall see later—a peasantry abundantly aware of its rights, canny about local political realities, and far from blinded by ignorance or superstition. Not that European peasants were somehow heroic and enlightened by the standards of twentieth-century observers; they were self-interested, short-run maximizers like other people. But they were not stupid, stolid, fanatical, servile, fiercely attached to particular plots of land or blindly committed to traditional ways of cultivating them. Except when they had to be. That old portrait of the European peasantry sprang from the brushes of aristocrats and bourgeois who thereby explained the resistance of the rural population to having its land, labor, and capital subordinated to the needs of international markets and national states.

The situation of European peasants differed in important regards from that of their counterparts in other major peasant areas such as China, Japan, and India. For one thing from the time the Roman Empire disbanded they were never subject to the rule of a single large political structure. Before the emergence of multiple national states lay a period of even greater political fragmentation among principalities, bishoprics, city-states, and other small structures. As a consequence, at any given time the European peasantry as a whole was experiencing a wide variety of fiscal policies, demands for military service, legal systems, forms of political control.

Again, corporate structures were relatively weak among European peasants. Although toward the south and east of Europe there was some tendency for agglomeration into large, complex households and for the emergence of solidary lineages, in general, European peasants settled for weakly patrilineal systems of inheritance, traced kinship through shifting and loosely bounded bilateral kindreds, and built their households of nuclear or stem families, temporarily augmented or depleted as a function of the nuclear family's current labor supply.

If European peasants lived with weak corporate structures, they compensated to some degree by building exceptionally strong communities. By strength I do not mean harmony or solidarity, but two other things: first, the extent to which the local population as such exerted collective control over local land, labor, and capital; second, the extent to which the local population acted as an entity in pursuit of its members' common interests. The interaction with expanding states gave a temporary boost to the peasant community's capacity for collective action outside its own ambit. Its employment as an instrument of tax collection, for example, probably added to the community's extractive powers. It even added, paradoxically, to the community's short-run capacity to resist unjust taxation.

The exceptional control of European peasant communities over local land, labor, and capital showed up in such arrangements as communal regulation of planting, harvesting, gleaning, pasturage, and disposition of crops. It also took the form of collective regulation of marriage, settlement, religious practice, and exchange of labor among households, although these controls were weaker and more variable than those directly touching the use of the community's land. Very likely the earlier importance of the manor as the unit of settlement, the prevalence of concentrated villages instead of hamlets or isolated farms, and the predominant organization of religious practice within well-defined parishes all contributed to the relative strength of European peasant communities.

As compared with peasantries in most of the world, the European peasantry was quite homogeneous. Only China had so little linguistic variation over so large a population and so large an area. Kinship patterns, legal practices, religious forms, agricultural routines, annual cycles, folklore, perhaps even life plans were relatively uniform over a whole continent, by contrast with their variability in India, Southeast Asia, or the peasant sections of the Americas. As in China and Japan, the extension of a single empire over the entire region played a major part in the homogenization of peasant culture. The difference is that in Europe the empire disappeared for good, but the cultural forms associated with it survived.

This homogeneity was not so much a characteristic of the European peasantry as of the European population as a whole. The same is true of the final condition we must consider: the existence of a large-scale system of trade, markets, and economic interdependence

12

incorporating almost the entire territory of the continent. By the sixteenth century, for example, a well-defined division of labor was emerging between the grain-exporting regions of eastern Europe and the grain-importing, manufacturing areas of the Low Countries and southern England. The division of labor appeared on the commercial map, among other ways, in the role of Danzig as the outlet for wheat from the plains of Russia, Poland, and eastern Germany, in the role of Copenhagen as a point of transshipment and customs collection, in the role of Amsterdam as the great grain port of the West. Immanuel Wallerstein sums up the new arrangement by saying that the sixteenth century brought the emergence of a "European world-economy," in which England and Holland rapidly became the dominants, and which later extended its control to the entire world.

These, then, were the distinctive conditions in which the European peasantry acted through most of the period after 1500: political fragmentation, weak corporate structures, strong communities, cultural homogeneity, involvement in a large-scale system of economic interdependence and control. No one of these conditions sets off Europe from all other world areas of peasant predominance. But together they define a special situation. It is a situation in which landlords are relatively powerful *vis à vis* the political authorities, indeed often *are* the political authorities on a local or regional scale. It is a situation in which a political or economic invention—a form of taxation, a kind of military service, a reorganization of production—that works in one place is likely to be rapidly and cheaply transferable to other settings. It is a situation in which peasant communities (rather than kin groups, religious sodalities, secret societies, or the labor forces of particular productive organizations such as plantations or latifundia) are likely to be the principal vehicles of peasant collective action. It is a situation, finally, in which shifts in market relations to distant producers or consumers produce important changes in the welfare and interpersonal relations of the local peasant population.

Who Else Was There?

Suppose we adopt the idea of the rural population as the people living in settlements whose predominant activity is agriculture, regardless of size, location, or any of the other criteria sometimes used to distinguish rural from urban. From a theoretical and from a practical point of view, several elements of such a definition are problematic: (1) Who "lives in" a given place? How many transients, seasonal workers, individuals based there but working elsewhere shall we count? (2) What are the boundaries of a "settlement"? Shall we include the weavers' hamlet or the commercial center of a farming community? What of the village on its way to absorption into the suburbs of Zurich or Manchester? (3) How do we recognize a "predominant activity"? If three-fourths of the local population works on farms but three-fifths of the marketed output comes from textiles, what then?

We can easily invent working definitions to meet these difficulties. The point is that the choice of working definitions will determine our estimates of the rural population's composition. The more we confine the rural population to the people durably located in clusters of dwellings the majority of those occupants spend the majority of their time in agriculture, the higher we will raise our estimates of the proportion of the European rural population peasant, and the slower we will make the measured changes in the composition of the rural population. But the more we do so, the more we will also create "nonrural" populations living on farms or in small settlements in the midst of farms.

We will learn more, I think, by including everyone who spends a significant part of the year in a given place, by taking the lowest-level units in the political or marketing hierarchies as our settlements, and by letting the proportion of the community's total available time devoted to agriculture determine agriculture's predominance. The result of such criteria is to include a great many nonpeasants in the rural population, and to observe great, rapid fluctuations in both its size and its composition.

No occupational categories are independent of the social structures within which they operate. As a result, any set of general categories for the whole rural population will do violence to almost every particular rural area. With that warning, we may group Europe's rural population into the following rough categories: (1) landlords and managers, (2) commercial farmers, (3) peasants, (4) land-poor and landless agricultural laborers, (5) land-poor and landless industrial workers, (6) service workers, including professionals. The actual application of these categories to the sorting of rural populations will require the extensive use of statements beginning "To the extent that . . ."; e.g., to the extent that peasants specialize in cash crops but retain their control over the land, they become commercial farmers; to the extent that commercial farmers substitute labor hired from outside the household for labor within the household, they become landlords or managers. Furthermore, the overlap among the categories is often a more important social fact than the sheer numbers assignable to each of them; rural industrial workers, for example, often turned to agricultural wage-labor in seasons of peak demand, such as the harvest; peasants in regions with long dead seasons (such as the Alps) often doubled in woodcarving, clockmaking, schoolteaching, peddling, and other nonagricultural arts.

Many more distinctions are possible, sometimes essential; in much of western Europe, for example, it would confuse important issues to lump together domestic servants, hired hands, day-laborers and seasonal workers within the land-poor and landless. Nevertheless, the crude categorization catches the two fundamental distinctions in rural Europe: the directness of the individual's (or household's) involvement in exploitation of land, and the extent to which the individual (or household) depends for survival on the sale of labor power. A decline in the first is a large part of what we mean by industrialization. A rise in the second is the essence of what we mean by proletarianization.

Europe experienced great change along both dimensions during the five centuries after 1500. For the continent as a whole, the proportion of the rural population directly involved in the exploitation of land declined irregularly through the eighteenth century, then began to rise rapidly some time in the nineteenth. The dependence of the rural population on the sale of labor power rose significantly from 1500 until some time in the nineteenth century, then began a slow decline as all but the peasants and commercial farmers started to leave, but began to rise again in the twentieth century as capital-intensive agriculture squeezed out its small competitors. The earlier proletarianization occurred not only because landlords and managers consolidated their control over the land and squeezed peasants into wage labor, but also because rural manufacturing multiplied. There is another poorly understood origin of the proletariat: a natural increase in the eighteenth and nineteenth centuries that greatly exceeded the expansion of opportunities to work the land on one's own account. My own view is that the natural increase was initially a *consequence* of proletarianization, as individuals whose lives did not depend on peasant arrangements for inheritance and succession married younger and had more children. But there is little question that once the process got started two other things happened: (1) declining mortality also contributed importantly to the natural increase, (2) the multiplication of the rural proletarian population accelerated the proletarianization of the remainder of the rural population.

The Big Changes Behind

Behind the shifts in the rural population's composition lay massive changes in the organization of European social life. For present purposes, we need to keep our eyes on four interdependent transformations: statemaking, urbanization, industrialization, and commercialization.

Let us consider statemaking first. In 1500 Europe had a great many formally autonomous governments—about 500 by one count. They varied considerably in size and character: principalities, bishoprics, city-states, federations, empires, and a few entities already recognizable as weak national states. In the centuries that followed the number of formally autonomous governments shrank dramatically. Most contemporary maps of Europe outline about thirty-five separate entities, including such ministates as Monaco and San Marino. The great consolidation of governmental power occurred through military struggle and dynastic manipulation. The efforts to build the organization and assemble the resources for the struggle created large, centralized state apparatuses.

In the process, the managers of the state apparatus subordinated or absorbed the rival authorities within their subject territories, created routine ways of extracting resources from the population and extended the range of activities the state apparatus monitored and controlled. As this happened, national states became the dominant organizations in all of Europe. Looking back at the process, many nineteenth- and twentieth-century observers have felt it displayed a compelling and attractive logic—either because the presumed rationalization of politics represented by the national state was a fitting, inevitable accompaniment to the modernization of social life in general, or because heroes such as Louis XIV and Frederick the Great had a vision of the future, and the will to implement it. In reality, states took shape as a direct consequence of the efforts of competing sovereigns and their allies to increase their power to extract resources within their own territories and to command deference outside them. Over most of the period we are discussing, preparation for war was the principal state-building activity.

The national state was not, to be sure, the first concentration of power to impinge on the peasant's world. Earlier, warriors had used a combination of coercion, military protection, and material incentives to bring rural people under the control of the manor, even to the extent of making serfs of them. Churchmen and princes fed on vast, if scattered, rural domains. Trading cities (whether governed by churchmen, princes, or councils of freemen) characteristically extended their political power to their rural hinterlands. What was distinctive about the national state was its differentiation from other organizations, the specialization of its subdivisions, its territorial integrity, its scale, plus the scope and intensity of its claims on the subject population. Because national states were more effective warmaking machines than their competitors, they crowded organizations such as churches, trade federations, and noble families into the shadows. The dominance of national states in Europe was well established by the middle of the eighteenth century. The power of states relative to other organizations continued to grow long after that—at least until the emergence of mass parties and big corporations in the early twentieth century. The absolute power of states to command resources and compliance continues to increase in our own time; if a relative decline due to the competition from parties, corporations, unions, blocs of states, common markets, and other huge organizations has occurred, it has only happened recently and unemphatically. For close to five hundred years, European rural populations have felt the pressures of a more or less continuous statemaking process.

Statemaking mattered to rural collective action in more ways than one. First, the statemakers drew a large portion of the required resources directly from the countryside. That is most obvious with the rise of taxation and the expansion of military service. For Europe as a whole, the great bulk of tax revenues before the twentieth century came either from direct assessments of rural land or from levies on commodities regularly consumed by the rural population. When a rapid increase or an invention of a new tax occurred, it was usually in the one category or the other. As Gabriel Ardant has pointed out, when this insistent demand reached populations that were mainly engaged in subsistence agriculture, it put great pressure on them to market commodities that had previously been produced for local consumption only, or had been treated as part of the household capital: the cow, dairy products, garden crops, a piece of land. As Ardant does not point out, in predominantly peasant communities someone is likely to have a well-founded claim on any of the factors of production and any commodity or service produced locally; hence a new or expanded demand from the state ordinarily conflicts with someone's established right to the resources in question. The same is true of military conscription, which withdraws labor from the household and the community—the labor of young men, which is often crucial to the continuity of household or community. As we shall see, a great deal of rural collective action centered on taxation and conscription.

Statemaking also impinged on the countryside through the extension of routine administrative control into the village. The pace, timing, and effectiveness of administrative penetration varied widely from one part of Europe to another, but everywhere rural communities acquired governmental structures that were sanctioned, subsidized, monitored, reformed, and employed by higher authorities who were in turn directly or indirectly responsible to the state. A significant part of statemaking therefore consisted of the imposition of local governmental structures, the support of those who staffed them, and the implanting, supplanting, or absorption of local authorities. This

18

process, too, generated plenty of collective action in the countryside.

Finally, where states did not lay direct claims on resources, they regulated the use and transfer of resources. The best-documented case is the involvement of states in the production, consumption, and especially distribution of food. In the seventeenth and eighteenth centuries all European states created extensive apparatuses for the surveillance and assurance of the food supply of their cities, armies, and governmental personnel. To some degree, they all promoted the creation of national markets in food. By the nineteenth century states began to relax their direct controls over the distribution of food as rising agricultural productivity and improved shipping reduced the vulnerability of the nonagricultural population to starvation. From that point on, however, state involvement in production tended to increase; price supports, acreage allotments, marketing orders, and governmental certification of sensitive products became standard features of state policy. On balance, the involvement of states in food supply has increased steadily since the seventeenth century. Less visibly and less completely, the same trend holds for state regulation of the use of rural land, rural labor, and rural capital.

My account of statemaking stresses the costs to the peasantry, and neglects any benefits the rural population may have gained. If we were to prepare a giant balance sheet for the entire process, indeed, I think we would find peasants and the bulk of the rural population incurring large losses and few gains. In the long run, state promotion of marketing no doubt contributed to rising levels of rural living. State-supported development of education, transport, and communication eventually widened the range of intellectual and occupational opportunities available to people born in the country. Sooner or later, the governmental extension of policing and courts to rural areas probably reduced the exposure of countrymen to robbers, thieves, and bandits. In the long-run account, we must balance these advantages against the yielding of the bulk of the resources required by the entire statemaking process, and against a tremendous loss of local autonomy. In any case, the losses tended to be rapid, large, and visible, while the gains tended to be slow and invisible. For the history of rural collective action, the rapid, large, visible losses are far more important.

19

Urbanization

The urbanization of Europe helped transform the countryside by augmenting the demand for rural products, providing an outlet for rural labor, aiding the development of large organizations that imposed further controls over the countryside, and elaborating a system of communication linking rural areas with the rest of the world. By definition, it also shifted the relative bulk of the rural population. If by "urban" population we mean simply the population settled in predominantly nonagricultural places of a substantial size, Europe only began a strong, continuous drive to urbanization late in the eighteenth century. Before then there was plenty of urban growth, but at times the rural population grew faster than the urban population. Because the labor productivity of agriculture rose only slowly, because transport costs of foodstuffs and other urban necessities remained high, and because industry itself could take greater advantage of surplus rural labor by locating in the countryside, Europe as a whole did not even acquire the technical capacity to urbanize extensively until quite recently.

Exactly how did the urbanization of Europe happen? Any process of urbanization breaks down into three components: (1) net migration between rural and urban areas, the difference between total flows in one direction and total flows in the other; (2) differences in natural increase between rural and urban areas, which break down further into the balance between births and deaths in each set of areas; (3) the net transformation of existing settlements from urban to rural and rural to urban. In Europe as a whole, the natural increase of cities did not play a major part in urbanization until late in the nineteenth century. Indeed, the population in larger European cities probably suffered a natural decrease because of high mortality until some time after 1800. The transformation of existing rural settlements into urban ones (e.g., through a shift to predominantly nonagricultural production, or through incorporation of outlying agricultural villages into expanding cities) bulked larger throughout the period after 1500. But the major city-builder by far was migration out of rural areas. Between 1500 and 1900 (a period in which the population of Europe rose from 50-odd million to 400 million), net migration to cities from rural areas was on the order of 100 or 200

20

million people. Thus, the countryside participated directly in European urbanization; it supplied not only the food and the capital, but also the very people involved.

So far as I can tell from the risky data now available, the big-city population of Europe tripled during the sixteenth century, rose only a little during the seventeenth, doubled during the eighteenth century (especially after 1750), went up nearly ten times during the nineteenth century, and showed another brisk pace of increase during the twentieth. Some rough estimates of the proportion of the population in cities of 100,000 or more are:

1500	1.5%	1750	2.5
1550	2.0	1800	2.9
1600	2.8	1850	4.8
1650	2.4	1900	12.3
1700	2.4	1950	21.8

At the risk of explaining something that did not happen, I suggest that the seventeenth-century decrease occurred mainly because of the expansion of rural industry; the devastation of cities in war, especially the Thirty Years War, may also have played its part. During the eighteenth century the rural population increased so fast that the doubling of big-city population barely returned the proportion to its level of two centuries before. The decisive shift of the European population to cities did not begin until the spectacular growth of large, centralized, urban, job-providing organizations got underway after 1750.

In absolute terms, the rural population did not peak until long after that. Over Europe as a whole, more people probably lived in predominantly agricultural settlements than ever before; the absolute number did not begin to decline appreciably until late in the century. The population directly engaged in *agriculture* (as opposed to the population living in predominantly agricultural settlements) appears to have reached its peak around 1900, and only to have begun a significant decline in the 1930s. (The difference in timing between the decline of the rural population and the decline of the agricultural population is due to the fact that rural crafts, industries, services, and commerce declined before agriculture itself declined or became less labor-intensive.)

It is harder to trace the absolute numbers of peasants. That is partly because governments and researchers have not collected their population statistics with the distinction between peasant and non-peasant in mind, but mainly because the distinction itself refers to a location on a continuum rather than a neatly bounded category. My guesses are that: (a) in absolute numbers, peasants reached their European high point around 1800, only to decline rapidly thereafter and (b) Europe had far greater disparities in the pace and timing of the growth-decline of peasants than it did in fluctuations of rural population or population in agriculture. In much of eastern Europe, in southern England, in southern Spain, and perhaps in southern Italy as well, true peasants were already giving way in the seventeenth century, as large landlords consolidated their holdings, displaced peasant small holdings in favor of pasturage or large grain fields, and tilted the agricultural labor force toward landless and land-poor laborers. In France, northern Spain, much of Italy, the Alps, western and southern Germany, the Low Countries, Scandinavia, and the rest of the British Isles, on the other hand, peasants survived—sometimes even prospered—into the eighteenth and nineteenth centuries. In those areas (to simplify unconscionably) the peasant eventually disappeared along two rather different paths: into landless wage labor and into cash-crop farming.

Industrialization, Commercialization, and Capitalism

We can conveniently conceptualize industrialization as a two-dimensional shift of productive activity: out of primary industry into secondary and tertiary production; into larger and larger organizations:

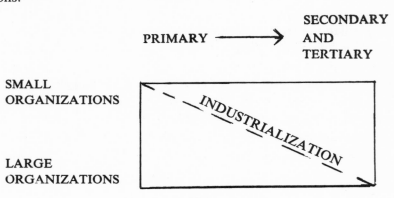

Before the French Revolution, Europe's industrial growth occurred mainly along the primary/secondary/tertiary dimension. Despite the development of the joint-stock company and other devices for pooling capital or labor, the average scale of the actual units of production may have declined as cottage industry and its equivalents flourished. The nineteenth-century growth of the factory, the corporation, the bureaucracy, and the twentieth-century emergence of large organizations in services, retail trade, construction, and agricultural products shifted the axis of change, without stopping the movement into secondary and tertiary industry.

These changes took place mainly in cities. Yet they had large impacts on the countryside. They generated unparalleled demands for capital, labor, agricultural products, and, eventually, land; a significant share of all of these came from rural stocks. In most countries they also reduced the political weight of the countryside much more rapidly than the sheer decline of rural numbers would have led anyone to expect; the political advantage went to those who controlled large organizations.

The commercialization of European production preceded the dramatic growth in scale, and accompanied the shift toward secondary and tertiary industry. By commercialization I mean the increasing subjection of the factors of production and of the goods and services produced to market control. The process is again two-dimensional: markets increase in scale, the range of resources subject to their control expands. Both changes were transforming the European countryside throughout the period we have been considering. But the pace and timing of commercialization varied enormously by region and resource. By the end of the eighteenth century, for example, northeastern France, the Low Countries, northwestern Germany, and southern England had already built a large-scale market in grains, while the surrounding areas marketed much less of their grain, and on a smaller scale. The same commercialization of the grain market had occurred in the immediate hinterlands of major mercantile, industrial, and administrative centers elsewhere: Milan, Barcelona, Moscow, and so on. In a different way, but almost to the same degree, the grain-producing areas of Hungary, Poland, eastern Prussia, and other sections of eastern Europe began a significant commercialization of their production in the sixteenth century. On the other hand, the areas of thoroughgoing peasant production were —almost by definition—areas in which commercialization proceeded slowly and late.

Commercialization and industrialization together produce capitalism in the classic Marxist sense of the term. E. J. Hobsbawm puts it this way:

> For Marx the conjunction of three phenomena is necessary to account for the development of capitalism out of feudalism: first . . . a rural social structure which allows the peasantry to be "set free" at a certain point; second, the urban craft development which produces specialized, independent, nonagricultural commodity production in the form of the crafts; and third, accumulations of monetary wealth derived from trade and usury. [Hobsbawm, 1964, p. 46]

Out of these conditions, according to Marx, emerged a system of production for exchange-value (instead of use) performed mainly by wage-workers under the direction of persons who controlled means of production requiring substantial capital investments: capitalism. Capitalist industry and capitalist agriculture were both, by these standards, well launched in the seventeenth century, but only under full sail in the nineteenth and twentieth. Without acute discomfort, we can describe the entire process from the seventeenth century onward as the penetration of capitalism into the European countryside.

The balance sheet we draw up for the peasant experience under commercialization and industrialization depends on the relative values assigned to material well-being and the control over one's own means of production. On the count of material well-being, there is little evidence of significant improvement (and some evidence of significant decline) for the rural population as a whole before the late eighteenth century. The important, continuous amelioration of food, clothing, shelter, and health care only dates from the late nineteenth century. For the peasant segment that remained peasant, improvement began earlier. On the count of control over the means of production, the experience of the rural population as a whole was an almost continuous decline from the sixteenth century to the nineteenth- and twentieth-century exodus of rural proletarians. In the process, a minority of the peasants stayed peasants, and on the average probably experienced improvements in material welfare from late in the nineteenth century; another minority left the peasantry for cash-crop farming, and very likely improved its lot more or less continuously from the sixteenth century onward; and the majority passed out of the peasantry into the rural or urban proletariat, experiencing permanent losses of control over production and at least short-run declines in material well-being. For this majority, the penetration of capitalism into the countryside offered plenty of causes for complaint.

Rural Collective Action

Collective action, broadly conceived, consists of the application of pooled resources to common ends. Collective action runs the whole range from continuous, high coordinated actions (such as a professional association's initiation of a letter-writing campaign) to discontinuous, uncoordinated actions (such as a crowd's attack on the symbols of an unpopular regime). Here I want to concentrate on the discontinuous end of the range, and on the actions of ordinary rural people rather than of elites or governments.

At this end of the range, it is useful to distinguish among three big classes of collective actions: competitive, reactive, and proactive. The distinctions depend on the claims the collective actors are asserting in their actions. *Competitive* actions lay claim to resources also claimed by other groups which the actor defines as rivals, competitors, or at least as participants in the same context. For example, Elina Haavio-Mannila has studied the institutionalized village fights which prevailed in rural Finland up to the end of the nineteenth century. The combatants usually consisted of two previously organized male fighting gangs, each representing a specific locality. The fighting reinforced the claims of the victors to control of the marriageable females within their villages, to dominance in their own territories, and to a kind of deference from the rest of the population. Some version of the village fight was commonplace almost everywhere in Europe.

Events such as the village fight appear inconsequential in retrospect. They did not start wars or bring down regimes. Yet people took them seriously, and many died in them. In general form, they were similar to the frequent struggles of rival groups of artisans to seize control of each other's symbols or to disrupt each other's public ceremonies, as well as to the brawls that recurrently set soldiers and civilians, people from different linguistic or religious groups, or competing groups of students against each other. Such actions were generally shortlived and small in scale. In times of crisis, however, they could become long, large, and lethal.

Reactive collective actions consist of group efforts to reassert established claims when someone else challenges or violates them. In a standard European scenario, a group of villagers who had long pastured their cattle, gathered firewood, and gleaned in common fields found a landlord or local officials—more likely, the two in collaboration—fencing the fields by newly acquired or newly declared right of property; the villagers commonly warned against the fencing; if the warning went unheeded, they attacked the fences and the fencers. The villagers acted in the name of rights they still considered valid. The same basic outline applies to the bulk of European food riots, tax rebellions, local actions against military conscription, and machine-breaking. Reactive actions usually remained quite local in scope. But occasionally, as in England's "Swing" riots of 1830 or the French "Flour War" of 1775, they covered whole regions and stirred up whole countries.

Proactive collective actions assert group claims that have not previously been exercised. We are familiar with the demonstration: in its pure form, a named group appears in a public place, displays its identify and its grievances, affiliations, or demands via symbols, placards and banners, voices them in speeches, chants, shouts, or songs, and identifies the person or group to whom the message is addressed by means of physical location, symbolic action, or explicit statement. Although it had important predecessors, the demonstration came into its own as a way of doing public business with the mass electoral politics of the nineteenth century. The strike, the sponsored public meeting, the seizure of premises by an insurrectionary committee, the petition drive are other common proactive forms.

Let me clarify one point that is likely to cause trouble. Strictly speaking, a strike or a demonstration could fall into any of the three types: competitive, reactive, or proactive. The decision depends not on the form of the action but on the claims being asserted. European workers have often struck, in fact, as a way of defending job rights that were threatened by employers; those strikes were reactive. Yet there is a general association between proaction and strike activity: since the early nineteenth century, workers who have asserted new claims have commonly done so via the strike, and a substantial majority of strikes have asserted new claims. Roughly the same sort of statement applies to demonstrations, public meetings, and the like. Thus, it is a shorthand—but one that will do no harm once we understand it—to speak of the food riot as a reactive form of collective action and the strike as a proactive form.

The proactive forms become dominant (in terms of numbers of people involved and in terms of political significance) in something like the same rhythm as drummed out the reactive forms. The idea that one immediately replaced the other, however, is an illusion. The illusion is due to the fact that proactive forms of collective action were building up in European urban areas in the nineteenth century as the reactive forms declined in rural areas. If we consider the countryside alone, we discover a rather different situation: (1) in general, a long lull of inactivity appeared in rural areas between the last surges of reactive collective action and the first extensive proactive stirring; (2) in most of rural Europe the scope and intensity of proactive movements never came close to the scope and intensity of their reactive predecessors.

Why the shift from competitive to reactive to proactive? Broadly speaking, the reactive forms began to predominate in the European countryside after 1600 because of statemaking, urbanization, and the growth of capitalism. Each of these processes impinged on the rural population as a series of claims on resources—land, labor, commodities—that were already committed to local ends by well-established rights and routines. Country people fought back. They tried to withhold young men from military service, money, crops, or livestock from the tax collector, land from the enclosing landlord. They did so in the name of established rights.

Other conditions also made a collective response more likely than passive resistance, individual bargaining, or grumbling capitulation: the strength of local organization, the availability of allies, the weakness of the authorities, the weight of the prior claims on the resources in question, the acuteness of the current need for them. Food riots came with food shortages, all right; the point is that in times of shortage they only occurred where and when the users of a local market had a well-established prior right to grain produced or stored locally, and that right seemed threatened by the failure of the local authorities to act against hoarders, speculators, gougers, or exporting merchants. As the demand for marketed grain stepped up in the cities and in the armies, more and more local authorities found themselves caught between the desire of merchants to export and the insistence of the local population that their rights came first. In similar ways, the other reactive forms of collective action became prevalent as the demands of city, state, and national market impinged on the countryside.

Why, then, did the reactive forms ever disappear? Mainly, I think, for two reasons: (1) because the repressive power of European governments in the countryside increased during the nineteenth century; (2) because the local organization on which the collective action was based disintegrated as capitalism transformed the countryside. In western Europe, at least, state-backing policing of rural areas via such specialized forces as gendarmerie, constabulary, and carabinieri greatly expanded during the nineteenth century. Prior to that expansion, local authorities had to rely on militias and on detachments of the regular army when they wanted to check collective action by force; they had a great deal of discretion as to taking any action at all. The professionalization of policing means that a force that was experienced in crowd control and responsive to directives from outside the local community patrolled the countryside regularly. Combined with the technical assistance of the telegraph, the railroad, and the expanded governmental bureaucracy, the growth of rural policing multiplied the state's involvement—and the state's effectiveness—in checking rural collective action.

The other side is the disintegration of the local organization on which the reactive claims were based. As rural crafts lost ground, so did the structures that united the craftsmen. As migrants streamed out of the countryside, their home communities lost the young people who would previously have stood in the front ranks. As the rural poor grew poorer, they committed their remaining energies and resources to survival. As peasants stopped being peasants, the specific commitment of each day of household labor, of each garden patch, of each bushel of rye to some segment of the common enterprise declined. As a consequence, the rural population's capacity and propensity for collective action diminished.

Eventually, however, proactive movements arose in some parts of the European countryside. In the Po Valley, the landless laborers on big farms were already making wage demands and organizing strikes in the 1870s. At the same time, small holders and rural craftsmen of Andalusia were forming into syndicates, affiliating with the anarchist movement, and making demands for a say in prices, wages, and working conditions. Thirty years later winegrowers of Champagne marched through Reims demanding a fair price for their products. Specialized associations—cooperatives, *fasci,* unions, and others—generally lay behind these actions. The associations drew disproportionately on relatively skilled rural workers and farmers whose entire welfare depended on the market price of labor or of the commodities they produced; they were not the doing of peasants, of the very poor, of the floating population. The associations were commonly homogeneous in class composition and often established alliances with other associations (not necessarily of the same class composition) elsewhere. They contended over national policies, national markets, and national structures of power to a degree unseen in the earlier reactive waves of collective action. How they came into being is one of the major themes in this paper's final sections.

Rural Violence in Italy, Germany, and France

Collective actions that lead to violence are not representative of all forms of collective action. But the use of violence as a sort of marker for the event we want to trace increases the likelihood that both published sources and archives will contain detailed information concerning the events. That is both because damage of persons or objects (which is what I mean by violence) attracts the attentions of

29

authorities and reporters, and because the violence is commonly a direct consequence of the intervention of authorities in what otherwise would have been a nonviolent collective action; by and large, the involvement of officials of large organizations, including states, in an event greatly increases the volume of documentation the event leaves behind. Furthermore, the violent events typically appear as members of strings of actions that are quite similar, but mainly nonviolent: strikes, meetings, demonstrations, angry gatherings, and so on. The occurrence of the violence in one member of the string tends to make the entire string visible. Thus an enumeration procedure that searches for violent events singles out relatively well-documented instances of collective action, but still has a fair chance of providing a first approximation of the general character of the discontinuous collective action going on in different places and periods.

In Italy the larger-scale collective violence between the departure of Napoleon and the Revolution of 1848 was mainly urban; the most notable events were scattered attempts by small groups of liberal conspirators to take over one capital or another. The first widespread rural conflicts came with Lombardy's food riots of 1846. They consisted mainly of blockages—attempts to keep grain from moving out of a community on its way to market. The Lombardy food riots coincided with similar events in France, Germany, Spain, and other parts of western Europe, all hit with poor harvests and high prices.

The Revolution of 1848 brought more food riots, numerous attacks on tax collectors, and a spate of land invasions. The land invasions of both north and south saw the rural population repossessing commons and former peasant lands that bourgeois landlords had bought up. Although another round of food riots arrived in 1853, the next large-scale rural conflicts began with Garibaldi's drive up from the south in 1860. The land invasions, attacks on mills, brigandage, and tax rebellions that occurred in Sicily, Apulia, Basilicata, and elsewhere were marvelously ambivalent: apparently pro-Unification before the unifiers had cemented their power, apparently anti-Unification afterward. The change occurred not so much in the objectives the rural population itself was seeking as in the allies and enemies it acquired by seeking them. In the areas of weakest central control —notably Sicily—the conflicts continued through the 1860s.

In 1868 and 1869 the passage of a national milling tax, the *macinato,* excited movements against mills, municipalities, and tax collectors in the major areas of rural wage labor. The tax survived, and the attacks recurred into the 1890s. But in the 1870s a rather different kind of action spread: the strike of agricultural workers such as the ricegrowers of the Po Valley. From then until the Fascists consolidated their power, the laborers' strike was the predominant form of large-scale rural collective action in Italy. In Sicily from 1891 to 1894, however, the organizations called *Fasci* ("bundles" in the sense of groupings giving solidarity and strength) multiplied. They engaged in repeated local efforts to insure better contracts for share-croppers and tenant farmers, to get higher wages for agricultural laborers and to reduce consumption taxes. The movement fell to pieces in the bloody repression of 1894.

From that point on, the predominant forms of collective action in rural Italy did not change significantly for some time. There were recurrent food riots, but now they were less often old-fashioned blockages or efforts to seize temporary control of the local market than demonstrations in which food prices figured as major griev-ances. There were land invasions in the south when the central power weakened, as in 1919–20. The actions that brought the Fascists to power were chiefly urban (in fact, they consisted especially of Fascist attacks on the headquarters and personnel of organized labor). That generalization, however, requires two significant qualifications: (1) the first targets of the city-based Fascist squads were the organized agricultural workers of the Po Valley; (2) rural workers did take part in the abortive general strikes against the Fascist takeover. Autono-mous rural collective action on any scale disappeared under the Fascists. After World War II it reappeared in its classic form: agricultural strikes, land occupations, demonstrations about taxes and prices.

In Germany as well as Italy the large-scale collective action of the early nineteenth century was strongly concentrated in cities. The years 1830–31 and 1845–47 brought their rounds of rural food riots, the famous weavers' revolt of 1844 involved many rural workers, and the recurrent actions of the 1830s and 1840s against enclosing land-lords and purchasers of village commons certainly drew in country people. Yet they were exceptions. Germany's only substantial break in governmental continuity came with the revolutions of 1848, which brought the expected antitax movements, food riots, and actions against enclosing landlords, plus more peculiarly German religious conflicts including attacks on Jews. After that point, the paths of Germany and Italy ran in quite different directions. Except for the special case of mining regions, rural areas thereafter figured only slightly in German collective violence, probably of collective action in general. Religious conflicts recurred into the twentieth century, rights to forests formerly held in common continued to generate conflict up to World War I, and food riots persisted past 1848. Germany, however, experienced nothing like the massive movements of Italian agricultural workers. Like the Fascists, the Nazis concentrated their destructive work in the cities where socialists, communists, and organized workers clustered. As in Italy, once the authoritarian party had seized power autonomous rural collective action simply disappeared.

France provides a third experience for scrutiny. The rural collective violence of the earlier nineteenth century there has many points in common with that of Germany and Italy: a prevalence of food riots, antitax movements, invasions of former common lands. In the French revolutions of 1830 and 1848 we can see an interesting pattern: a first stage strongly concentrated in the major cities, as the insurgents seize the instruments of national government; a second stage more widely dispersed over the country, as the new regime attempts to re-establish effective central control and encounters unexpected resistance. The resistance (most dramatically in rebellions against new taxes) did not necessarily mean that the countryside had remained or had become counterrevolutionary, but that the agenda of the city-based revolutionaries differed from the agendas of their rural counterparts. A sort of extrapolation and transfiguration of the pattern occurred in 1851, when large segments of the French rural population rose against the coup d'état of Louis Napoleon. That was the last large-scale collective action of the countryside for many years.

In the 1890s, small holders and agricultural laborers—especially winegrowers—appeared on the French national scene. They organized, demonstrated, and struck with increasing frequency into the twentieth century. Their movement receded after 1907, and only reappeared on a large scale in the 1930s. Then the winegrowers found themselves in the company of dairy farmers and other producers; they joined national agrarian parties and political movements to a larger degree than they had before World War I. In the 1950s and 1960s producers' actions again dominated the rural scene: coordinated withholding of crops, ceremonious dumping of milk or potatoes in public places, well-publicized roadblocks, demonstrations demanding price supports. By this time, well-organized national pressure groups were speaking in the name of, if not always with the support of, "the peasantry" of France.

In Italy, Germany, and France alike a significant shift from reactive to proactive forms of collective action occurred in the countryside during the nineteenth and twentieth centuries. In all three countries, the movement of common land into private hands, the granting of priority to the national market, and the imposition of consumption taxes fueled conflict after conflict in rural areas. In the three countries the major transfers of power at the national level produced parallel struggles on a smaller scale in the countryside. Yet there are important differences among France, Italy, and Germany. Most notably, agricultural laborers organized and sustained a high level of collective action over a long period in Italy, played a lesser but still detectable part in French agrarian movements, and figured little in German collective action at any time past the revolutions of 1848.

Peasants, in the strict sense of the word, contributed rather less to the collective actions we have reviewed than did other members of the rural population. In the nineteenth century rural industrial workers and agricultural laborers were volatile. In the twentieth century the rural industrial workers had practically disappeared, but agricultural laborers continued their action for a while, and cash-crop producers became increasingly active. This summary holds best for France. Still, in none of the three countries were peasants the major rural actors.

My enumeration of events is misleading in one regard. It suggests that two main types of people—commercial farmers and proletarians —organized and acted. Such a summary slights the importance of peasants who were undergoing proletarianization. Remember the main paths out of the peasantry: (1) into rural wage labor (either agricultural or manufacturing), (2) into urban wage labor (typically service industries), (3) into commercial farming. In Europe peasants who found themselves on the path into rural wage labor, but still had some claims on the land, seem to have had a special propensity to struggle. Their determination made a difference at two distinct points in the process of proletarianization. The first was the earlier round of struggles over enclosures, subdivision of common lands, farming out of forests, and other transfers of what had been public property into private ownership. The people who fought hardest, so far as I can tell, were those who were surviving as peasants by means of those supplementary rights of grazing, gleaning, woodgathering, and so on. The invaders of fields and forests were commonly landholders of a sort, but holders of too little land to support a family without supplementary access to common resources. No doubt a substantial number of these people were already selling some of their household labor to survive; the suppression of common rights accelerated their proletarianization. So did the insistence that they find the cash to pay consumption taxes, and the increasing reluctance of local officials to subsidize the price of food and regulate its distribution in times of shortage and high prices. They reacted.

At a later stage in the process of proletarianization, we find peasants (or semipeasants) who have managed to survive the first round of capitalist transformation by shifting to cash-crop production. Some of them are on their way out of the peasantry into viable commercial farming. Many of them, however, find their specialized skills undercut by competition from big producers. The best-documented examples I know are in winegrowing. In the village of Cruzy (Hérault), Harvey Smith shows us the shift of agriculture toward winegrowing as the railroads expanded the available markets after 1850, the rise of a class of specialists in winegrowing who typically made a living from their own small landholdings in addition to (or after) hiring out their labor to others, the disintegration of their position as the larger landholders reoriented production toward cheaper wines and toward work routines requiring less skill. They fought, too: by organizing syndicates, by setting up cooperatives, by

34

joining national protests. The most interesting feature of their activity was their coalition with the relatively unskilled laborers who were, in a sense, destroying them. These "agricultural artisans" provided the organizational nucleus of the laborers' movement. Likewise, Temma Kaplan shows us the sherry-producing small holders, threatened with proletarianization, at the center of the ostensibly proletarian anarchist movement of Jerez de la Frontera. In fact, this combination of a nucleus of skilled but threatened workers with a larger mass of unskilled workers in closely related employment seems to have been the best guarantee of large-scale militancy in nineteenth-century Europe—whether in agriculture or in manufacturing.

Peasant Movement

In some conditions, then, European peasants did play a significant part in rural collective action. Would it be proper, however, to speak of European peasant *movements* during the last two centuries? In his useful discussion of the concept "social movement," Paul Wilkinson lays out three criteria:

> 1. A social movement is a deliberate collective endeavor to promote change in any direction and by any means, not excluding violence, illegality, revolution, or withdrawal into "utopian" community . . .
> 2. A social movement must evince a minimal degree of organization, though this may range from a loose, informal or partial level of organization to the highly institutionalized and bureaucratized movement and the corporate group . . .
> 3. A social movement's commitment to change and the *raison d'être* of its organization are founded on the conscious volition, normative commitment to the movement's aims or beliefs, and active participation on the part of the followers or members . . . [Wilkinson, 1971, p. 27]

The three criteria—orientation to change, organization and normative commitment—have a refreshing simplicity and workability. They contrast nicely with the frequent efforts of theorists to make the unrealism of the group's ends or the illegitimacy of its chosen means set off social movements from other forms of collective action. If we consider collective action to be any application of pooled resources on behalf of common ends, then a social movement is a special kind of sustained collective action: it is collective action in which organized groups of committed people deliberately seek to promote change. A peasant movement, then, is simply such an effort in which the members are, or perhaps claim to be, predominantly peasant.

Orientation to change, organization, normative commitment: the whole tone of the definition is proactive, rather than competitive or reactive. If we are to remain faithful to the definition, and hold on to a strict rendering of the word "peasant," then the message of the previous analysis is straightforward: a peasant movement is nearly a contradiction in terms. European peasants have often engaged in collective action, but almost always in the competitive or reactive modes. The rural population of Europe has mounted a substantial amount of proactive collective action, but the actors have typically been nonpeasants. The major exception appears to be peasants who are undergoing proletarianization. Not only do they often resist in a sustained and organized fashion, but they sometimes transform themselves from defensive to offensive actors.

The rarity of proactive collective action and of true social movements among European peasants, however, does not mean that they completely lacked revolutionary potential. On the contrary, the European experience reveals the revolutionary potential of reactive peasant actions such as resistance to taxation and occupation of lost lands. In combination (and sometimes in conscious coalition) with the laying of new claims by bourgeois and workers in city and country, these ostensibly nonrevolutionary peasants helped achieve almost all of the nineteenth-century revolutions in France, Germany, and Italy; they played a significant part elsewhere in Europe. From the point of view of a thoroughgoing revolution (as Gramsci saw long ago), the difficulty was not that the peasantry lacked the capacity to act, but that the peasant-worker coalition was usually too fragile to endure much beyond the toppling of the previous regime. In most nineteenth-century revolutions the peasants fell out of the revolutionary coalition with workers and left-wing bourgeois even faster than the workers did. They helped produce a transfer of power but failed to retain a share of control over the new power. And as the new regime sought to reimpose old obligations, substitute new ones, or avoid the execution of promises made to peasants in the first heady days of the struggle, the peasants often reacted again. Hence their thoroughly reactionary reputation.

Here we rejoin the insights of Eric Wolf's *Peasant Wars of the Twentieth Century*. Wolf portrays a peasantry beset by capitalism which first acts to defend itself against encroachments on its land, its labor, its commodities, its capital. In doing so, Wolf's peasantry sometimes moves over into a direct attack on its exploiters, real or imagined. It sometimes forms alliances with urban revolutionaries, and thus helps achieve a national transfer of power. Wolf's peasantry is a tragic figure, likely to withdraw from active involvement in the alliance once the threat to its own resources has been overcome, yet likely to be destroyed by the success of the revolution it has helped accomplish. For the world as a whole remains capitalist, and the logic of a capitalist world is to transform peasants into proletarians.

REFERENCES

Ågren, Kurt, Gaunt, David, Erikssen, Ingrid, Rogers, John, Norberg, Anders, and Åkerman, Sune
  1973 *Aristocrats, Farmers, Proletarians.* Essays in Swedish Demographic History. Uppsala: Scandinavian University Books.

Ardant, Gabriel
  1971–1972 *Histoire de l'impôt.* Paris: Artheme Fayard. 2 vols.

Basile, Antonio,
  1958 "Moti contadini in Calabria dal 1848 al 1870." *Archivio storico per la Calabria e Luciana,* 27:67–108.

Berkner, Lutz K.
  1972 "Rural family organization in Europe: a problem in comparative history." *Peasant Studies Newsletter,* 1:145–55.

Bleiber, Helmut
  1969 "Bauern und Landarbeiter in der bürgerlich demokratischen Revolution von 1848/49 in Deutschland." *Zeitschrift für Geschichtswissenschaft,* 17:289–310.

Blok, Anton
  1973 *The Mafia of a Sicilian Village, 1860–1960.* New York: Harper and Row.

Chayanov, A. V.
  1966 *The Theory of Peasant Economy.* Homewood, Ill.: Richard C. Irwin.

Del Carria, Renzo
  1966 *Proletari senza rivoluzione: Storia delle classe subalterne italiane dal 1860 al 1954.* Milan: Oriente. 2 vols.

Della Peruta, Franco
  1953 "I contadini nella rivoluzione lombarda del 1848." *Movimento operaio,* n.s., 5:525–75.

Diaz del Moral, Juan
  1967 *Historia de las agitaciones campesinas andaluzas—Córdoba.* Madrid: El Libro del Bolsillo. 2d ed.

Gramsci, Antonio
  1949 *Il risorgimento.* Turin: Einaudi.

Haavio-Mannila, Elina
1958 "Village fights. A sociological study of the Finnish village fight institution." Reprint of English summary of *Kylätappelut.* Helsinki: Porvoo.

Hobsbawm, E. J.
1959 *Primitive Rebels.* Manchester: Manchester University Press
1962 *The Age of Revolution. Europe 1789–1848.* London: Widenfeld and Nicholson.
1964 "Introduction" to Karl Marx, *Pre-Capitalist Economic Formations.* London: Lawrence and Wishart.

Hobsbawm, E. J., and Rudé, George
1969 *Captain Swing.* London: Lawrence and Wishart.

Kaplan, Temma
1975 "The Social Base of Nineteenth Century Andalusian Anarchism in Jerez de la Frontera." *Journal of Interdisciplinary History,* vol. 6.

Koselleck, Reinhart
1967 *Preussen zwischen Reform und Revolution.* Stuttgart: Klett.

Palloix, Christian
1971 *L'économie mondiale capitaliste.* Paris: Maspéro. 2 vols.

Pomponi, Francis
1972 "Emeutes populaires en Corse: Aux originies de l'insurrection contre la domination gênoise (Décembre 1729–Juillet 1731)." *Annales du Midi,* 84:151–81

Poussou, Jean-Pierre
1971 "Les mouvements migratoires en France et à partir de la France de la fin du XVe siècle au début du XIXe siècle: Approches pour une synthèse." *Annales de Démographie Historique,* 1970. Paris: Mouton.

Procacci, Giuliano
1964 "Geografia e struttura del movimento contadino della valle padana nel suo periodo formativo (1901–1906)." *Studi storici,* 5:41–120.

Romano, Salvatore Francesco
1959 *Storia dei Fasci siciliani.* Bari: Laterza.

Smith, Denis Mack
1968 *A History of Sicily. Modern Sicily after 1713.* London: Chatto and Windus.

Smith, J. Harvey
1972 "Village Revolution: Agricultural Workers of Cruzy (Hérault), 1850–1910." Doctoral dissertation in history, University of Wisconsin.

Tilly, Louise A.
1972 "La révolte frumentaire, forme de conflit politique en France."
Annales; Economies, Sociétés, Civilisations, 27:731–57.

Tilly, Richard
1970 "Popular Disorders in Germany in the Nineteenth Century: A
Preliminary Survey." *Journal of Social History,* 4:1–41.

Wallerstein, Immanuel
1974 *The Modern World-System. Capitalist Agriculture and the Origins
of the European World-Economy in the Sixteenth Century.* New York:
Academic Press.

Wilkinson, Paul
1971 *Social Movement.* London: Macmillan.

Wolf, Eric
1969 *Peasant Wars of the Twentieth Century.* New York: Harper and
Row.

Peasant Mobilization in Twentieth-Century Bengal

J. H. BROOMFIELD*

The Naxalites

IN THE SUMMER OF 1967 YOUNG MARXIST LEADERS OF A PEAS-
ant association in Naxalbari in North Bengal organized an agitation
to prevent rural landlords, dispossessed under land reform legislation, from retaining control of their property through the falsification
of transfer deeds. Demonstrations against the offenders were accompanied in some places by the seizure of hoarded food grains and the
symbolic occupation of lands. The death of a policeman in one such
demonstration in late May was followed by police firing, and this in
turn provoked the agitators to violence against their opponents. The
state government, a Marxist-dominated coalition, was reluctant to
sanction strong measures to contain the movement, but finally in
July it agreed to act. Fifteen hundred armed police were poured into
the area, and within three weeks the agitation was smashed.

The movement had attracted attention throughout India, and considerable support, particularly among young intellectuals, in the
West Bengal capital, Calcutta. In the months that followed a new
Marxist party was organized with the leader of the North Bengal
agitation as its chairman, and the government Marxist "opportu-
nists" as its main target of criticism. The Naxalites, as the group was
called, espoused terrorist violence against the "people's oppressors,"
and called for support in a general uprising: "Today the basic task
is to liberate the rural areas through revolutionary armed agrarian
revolution and encircle the cities and, finally, to liberate the cities and

*This paper is dedicated to Dr. Sunil Kumar Sen, Professor of History, Rabindra Bharati
University, a veteran of the Tebhaga struggle. I am grateful for his sage guidance and warm
friendship during my 1971–73 research visit to Calcutta, when the ideas for this paper were
generated.

complete the revolution throughout the country."[1]

The immediate targets of Naxalite attacks were business and professional men, government officials and judges, and particularly policemen. The revolutionaries had remarkable success in 1969 and 1970 in terrorizing Calcutta and other West Bengal cities, from which the great majority of their members were drawn. By contrast they found they could not operate effectively in the countryside, where they met with general hostility. A number died at the hands of village mobs, and, once government resources were sufficiently organized to drive them from their Calcutta refuges, the movement was lost.

Country Versus City

This episode typifies efforts to mobilize the Bengal peasantry. Time and again in this century we find cases of urban-based intellectual radicals going out to seek support for a cause among the rural cultivators, and being rejected forcefully. As in this instance, they often moved to take advantage of apparently propitious disturbances in the countryside, and consequently were the more discountenanced by their failure. As also in this case, the advocacy and commission of violence was common, for violence is a well-worn (if not well-honored) tradition of Bengali political life—in the countryside as much as in the cities, as carpetbagging townsmen have found to their cost.

To understand these difficulties faced by Bengal's political elites we must take account of a striking demographic factor: in this region are juxtaposed one of the world's most dense and overwhelmingly agrarian populations, with one of the world's largest cities.[2] By the turn of this century Calcutta, with its twin Howrah, already had a million and a quarter people. Its population has continued to grow inexorably, if erratically, and is now close to eight million. Immense power and political opportunity was concentrated in Calcutta, particularly in the colonial period. It was the capital of British India through the first decade of the century; it remained thereafter the chief commercial, industrial, foreign trading, judicial, educational, and cultural center of the subcontinent. It was so much bigger and apparently so much more important than anything else in the region, the political scope it offered seemed so great, that many a Bengal politician was tempted to disregard all else. Calcutta could become a world in itself, demanding special political techniques, and giving in return its special rewards and its peculiar experience.

But Calcutta was not all in all. The great mass of Bengal's population and the largest part of its wealth lay in the rural hinterland, and this could not be neglected entirely. Even early in the century the imperatives of the nationalist movement—the desire to mobilize greater numbers in the struggle against the British—encouraged the leadership to hazard political forays outside the towns. The progressive extension of the franchise at approximately twelve-year intervals from 1909 made for a more sustained rural effort by both nationalists and their opponents, and provided a route for countrymen to enter institutional politics.[3]

The incentives existed, but the knowledge and skills to mobilize the peasantry were only slowly acquired. In particular there appears to have been a gulf of incomprehension at the complexity of rural society. Like so many academic historians, Bengal's urban-based politicians of the first quarter century spoke vaguely of the vast peasant masses, whom they alternately characterized as offering great radical potential or posing a fearful threat to the maintenance of ordered political life.

They were of course aware of, and seriously concerned with the problems posed by, the religious pluralism of the region. Bengal's population contained almost equal numbers of Hindus and Muslims, and a sizable minority of tribals, who were mostly Animists or Buddhists.

What the politicians appear not to have comprehended fully was the fierce strength of localism, which complicated the religious, as well as every other, problem of social and political integration. Bengal had no unified political tradition. Even under the Moguls, who, from the sixteenth to the eighteenth centuries, had incorporated most parts of north and central India under one rule, large areas of Bengal had remained in independent principalities. From the mid-eighteenth century Calcutta had increasingly acted as a metropolis for the entire region, but there was a concomitant growth of local antagonisms toward the great city, its dominant institutions and dominant elites.

The development of a network of navigation canals in the delta, and of the railways in the second half of the nineteenth century, extended Calcutta's influence in the hinterland, facilitating the movement of products and people to and from the city. This was counterbalanced, however, by the growth of new marketing and governmental centers, for the same period saw a great extension of the colonial administrative and judicial apparatus. Based in these growing rural towns (as they are aptly called in Indian English) were new local elites, composed mostly of parvenu families who had taken advantage of the entrepreneurial opportunities accompanying the improvement of transportation, the growth of the Calcutta and foreign markets, and the expansion of the bureaucracy.

The half century preceding World War I had seen the extension of Bengal's agricultural "frontier." The topography of the region had always hindered easy communication. Its shifting river courses, treacherous climate, and debilitating endemic diseases caused repeated local fluctuations in population densities and agricultural productivity. This meant that, even into the early years of the present century, there remained underutilized areas of Bengal and its fringe available for economic enterprise as transportation, agricultural, and health technologies were improved. New cash crops were introduced in many areas; trade in lumber became profitable; and fortunes were made in the mining of coal, clays, and minerals. Much of the capital for these extractive industries was generated from agriculture, and much of the profit was reinvested in agricultural land or, more exactly, in rent-producing rural tenures.[4]

Legal and Sociological Categories

Great scope for speculation in rents was provided by Bengal's notoriously complex land tenure system, a legacy of its patchwork political history.[5] To generalize grossly, there were five legal levels:

Raj—The State

Zamindar—Superior Landlord

Joatdar—Superior Tenure Holder

Raiyat—Cultivating Tenant

Bhagadar—Sharecropper

This structure, with its appearance of well-defined categories, and its impressive body of judicial and administrative documentation, has provided a continuing framework of analysis for economic and social historians. It is a snare and a delusion. The social realities of the Bengal countryside are obscured rather than illuminated by these legal classifications.

It is not surprising that academics, with their overweening regard for documents, should have been led astray; what is more remarkable is that Bengal's city politicians appear habitually to have fallen into the same error. Perhaps it is relevant that the majority were lawyers, members of another fraternity predisposed to rely on the written word. In justification of their equation of legal with social categories they could point to the presence in the rural towns of organizations bearing titles such as Zamindar Associations, Joatdar Societies, and Raiyat Cooperatives. The existence of these bodies tells us there were small-town or rural interest groups who found it useful to associate under a label recognized in the legal codes. It tells us little, however, about economic relationships and the exercise of power in the countryside.

Landlord, moneylender, peasant—here is an alternative and simpler categorization: the one customarily relied upon by the British, and the basis for their rural reform legislation. It proves no more helpful.

Acquisition of Power

What we must do, if we are to understand Bengal rural society as the groundwork for studying the history of peasant mobilization, is to look at the means by which power was acquired and held. What we find is a common pattern, albeit with infinite local variation, that cuts across the religious, caste, and legal divisions.

The first requirement was secure control, direct or indirect, of good arable land. This at the very least insured a supply of food for oneself, family, and other dependents in the recurrent times of scarcity. Frequently it also provided a surplus in those crises when the ability to supply or withhold food and seed grains gave one immense leverage with others. In an agrarian economy where formal credit institutions were at first nonexistent, and, when established, almost inaccessible because of bureaucratic red tape and corruption, the power of the man who could give quick loans of grain or money was great; and the opportunities for wealth equally great if one had sanctions to enforce the payment of outrageous rates of interest.

The most direct, if crude, sanction was the threat of violence to property or person, and the *lathial,* the club-wielding thug in the employ of a powerful man, is a ubiquitous figure in twentieth-century rural Bengal. To this day there is rivalry between localities as to which produces the best *lathials.* A more genteel procedure was to use the state-licensed *lathials*—the police—and the British had obligingly introduced a fine instrument of aggression—the land mortgage deed—which could be used to secure police assistance in the coercion of insubordinate debtors.

More subtle, but equally effective, was control of the processing and distribution of the basic agricultural commodity of an area. In most places this meant the husking and milling of paddy, its warehousing, and its transportation to a railway station or a river steamer landing.

Access to markets was obviously essential to agricultural producers; access to the administrative and judicial bureaucracy was almost equally important, and power was available to those who could control such access. There was a variety of means by which this might be done, ranging all the way from the use of carefully cultivated friendships, through bribery, to the most certain means of all: the acquisition of an appointment in the bureaucracy for oneself or a close relative. Patronage was the name of the game: a fascinating, seamless web in which a man was patron to many clients, and himself the client of more powerful men.

All these deadly serious games of power could be played at any level of rural society. The scale was different at different levels—or, to continue the game metaphor, the stakes were higher when the resources available to the players were greater—but the rules of the game were much the same at every level.

Now we can understand why it makes little sense to attempt to analyze rural society in terms of landlord, moneylender, and peasant.

These were not discrete roles. Ambitious cultivators with good land invariably used their surpluses to make loans to their neighbors and, if successful in accumulating more capital, they would most commonly invest in rent-producing or sharecropped lands. In favorable circumstances they could rapidly combine all three roles of peasant, moneylender, and landlord, and sustain those roles indefinitely. Moreover, the level of the tenure that they purchased depended less on its rank order in the legal hierarchy, than upon the access which it gave to good land and control of people on the land. In one instance it might be best to buy a *raiyati* tenure; in another, a *zamindari*. It all depended on the quality of the land and the human entanglements involved. This is why the legal categories can be so misleading, and why it is equally misleading to attempt to draw a line across the rural social order, and declare that those above it (*zamindars* and *joatdars* perhaps) were powerful, and those below (*raiyats* and *bhagadars)* powerless. Big men and little there were; fat cats and thin—but they were not ranked and neatly ordered.

Interestingly enough, the bigger men faced a problem that the smaller did not. To sustain their larger enterprise, they needed market and bureaucratic contacts at greater distances from their village base, in the towns and perhaps even in Calcutta. The danger was that they would lose that intimate contact with their locality indispensable for continued dominance in the highly personal world of peasant society, where rivals were always waiting to knock the feet out from under the successful man, and where today's clients could become tomorrow's agents of an enemy. Patronage may indeed be "lop-sided friendship,"[6] but in that asymmetry is great potential for enmity.

The successful man who moved his center of operations to the subdivisional or district town (to move any further afield was rarely expedient) could, if skillful, use his extended family, more distant kin, and hand-picked caste fellows to protect his interests in the home territory. An alternative was to depute a brother, cousin, son, or nephew to do the urban work. Whichever way the net was spread, it overlay and reinforced that other network of patron-clientage, binding village and rural town together in one system—and helping us comprehend the behavioral basis of the sustained strength of localism.

This description of the process by which power was gained and held will be misleading if it gives the impression that all individuals or groups had equal opportunities for mobility. That is patently incorrect, and the attention I have just given to the importance of family-kin-caste networks is the clue to the main area of inequality: some communities had preferred access to the bureaucracy because their kinsmen were the bureaucrats. For at least the first three decades of this century, the Hindu high castes enjoyed an overwhelming predominance at all levels of the administrative and legal systems in Bengal.

Peasant Mobilization?

Conservatism, and resistance to intrusions from the outside, are surely characteristic of a system such as this. How then can we expect to find peasant mobilization? With difficulty, is the short answer.

But there is a longer answer. Demography is again our point of departure. I have spoken of the extension of Bengal's agricultural "frontier" in the latter half of the nineteenth century. By the beginning of the second decade of this century, at the latest, all new lands had been fully occupied, and with widespread famine and epidemic disease better controlled, population numbers were climbing precipitously. The development of industry and other alternative sources of employment did not keep pace, and pressure on the land became intense. The numbers of landless grew, and hostilities in rural society increased proportionately.

This was the environment into which the nationalist movement intruded. It was at the end of World War I, with major constitutional reforms in prospect and a struggle under way for control of the Bengal organs of the Indian National Congress, that the first sustained effort was made to extend organization and recruitment to the rural towns. In the following four years, under Gandhi's national leadership, support was mobilized for a program of noncooperation, the aim being a total boycott of governmental institutions. The towns were the major arena of confrontation, but, given the networks linking town and village, the impact was felt in the countryside.

An example will illustrate this. In January 1921 in Midnapore

District, which lies to the southwest of Calcutta, the first elections were held for union boards, new local councils provided by the Bengal Village Self-Government Act of 1919. The electors were uncertain as to what they were voting for, but they had a vague idea that they were electing representatives to arbitrate village disputes and thus save lawyer and court fees. Many were dismayed when they discovered that they had, in fact, assisted in the formation of new bodies empowered to levy taxes. They were convinced that the urban people would use these to swindle them.

A local congressman, Birendra Nath Sasmal, saw his opportunity. He organized meetings at which he warned that the Village Self-Government Act opened the way for crushing taxation and other oppressions by the government. Resist now or forever be taxed, he declaimed. To win the all-important support of the small town elites, he used a factional rivalry. In the Contai subdivision, to which he belonged, the elite was divided into two groups: the locals and people from outside districts who had established themselves in practice in the Contai law courts and other professions. The legislative council and union board elections had been fought out between candidates of these two groups, and the "immigrants" had triumphed. Sasmal, who was a member of the dominant Mahishya caste, now took the leadership of the locals and carried them with him in his attack on the union boards.

The people were persuaded to refuse to pay taxes under the Village Self-Government Act, and the members of the boards were encouraged to reconsider the wisdom of their implementing the Act. By late June the Contai bazaar and walls along village roads carried inflammatory posters threatening the members with violence. Resignations soon followed, and those who held out had social and religious boycotts applied to them. Some were even prevented from securing labor to reap their paddy.

Having brought the operation of the union boards to a standstill in Contai, Sasmal turned his attention to other parts of Midnapore District, with similar success. By November the government was forced to admit that it would be better to suspend the Act than fight Congress on such shaky ground.

Throughout his campaign, Sasmal had been careful to draw a

distinction between the refusal of union board taxes, and that of land revenue taxes, for the latter were inextricably entwined with rent payments so essential a part of the income of his class of small town notables. In December 1921, however, he was imprisoned by the British, and the opposing Congress faction—the Gandhians—who had a more radical rural policy, stumped his district urging that the land tax be witheld. The peasants needed little persuading, for economically they had had a bad year and politically a very active one. As Sasmal and others had feared, they had their own ideas as to where the line should be drawn in the payment of tax: many were soon refusing all rent, to individual landlords as well as to the government. When, in some places, attempts were made to coerce them, landlords and their bailiffs were beaten. Such violence was becoming widespread, and, as a consequence, Gandhi called off the entire movement early in 1922. The political workers withdrew from the countryside, and the peasants were left to their fate.[7] Our historical records do not tell us what reprisals they suffered.

Voters and Associations

Congress's agitational campaigns were sporadic, though exceedingly important in spreading ideas and furnishing organizational models. Less dramatic but of more sustained significance were the elective institutions that had been expanded into the countryside in the same post-World War I period. The union boards were the lowest level in the system; the highest within Bengal was the provincial Legislative Council, to elect which over a million men had been enfranchised. There was heavy urban weightage, but the wealthy and a small percentage of the moderately prosperous in the countryside now had the vote.

The candidates for office were, as we might expect, those same powerful entrepreneurial figures who controlled the more extensive patronage networks, or their brokers, the small-town lawyers. The need to garner votes forced the candidates into alliances with other powerful figures, and some found it useful to formalize these alliances by forming "representative" voluntary associations with the misleading titles to which I referred earlier, namely, Joatdar Associations and Kisan Sabhas (Peasant Societies).

More important, because more comprehensive in their functions, were the caste associations. Some caste *sabhas* in Bengal dated from much earlier, but it was in the second and third decade of this century that many middle and lower castes were organizing.

The normal pattern of the new associations was for a handful of educated and professionally employed members residing in a district town or, more frequently, Calcutta to form a committee. Through printed circulars and at meetings called in the town most conveniently located for the majority of caste members, they explained the objectives of the proposed association. Typically, these included the improvement of the caste's ritual practices to conform with the higher status to which they claimed it was entitled. Stress was laid upon insuring that this "correct" ranking, and a caste name appropriate to it, be recorded at the decennial census. In some cases the abolition of endogamous subgroups within the caste was urged; in others, particularly where there was marked occupational differentiation between the divisions, a complete split was advocated. In view of the new powers vested in local councils and the provincial legislature, attention was drawn to the opportunities open to the caste if its members gave solid support to those of their fellows (usually the prime movers in the association) who were candidates for elective office. Caste members were urged to subscribe to make possible the educational campaign needed to effect these reforms, and to enable the association to provide aid for indigent caste members. Where the appeals were successful, the associations usually began the publication of caste journals, but few were sustained.[8]

In the Muslim community there was a similar reorganization and extension of the local Islamia Anjumans, which provided a vehicle from the mid-twenties for bitterly anti-Hindu and anti-Congress propoganda. Muslim voters were exhorted to support only those candidates who were committed to an attack on high-caste Hindu dominance, and the community as a whole was urged to take courage from its superior unity and its growing numerical superiority to resist the Hindus, with violence if need be. The 1930s and 1940s, decades of severe economic and political dislocation, give ugly evidence of the effectiveness of this teaching.

There was one leading Muslim politician, A. K. Fazlul Huq, who resisted the separatist trend. He foresaw the enfranchisement of additional large numbers of cultivators, and correctly predicted that support of a section of rural lower-caste Hindus, as well as Muslims, could be won by a politician who would advocate restrictions on the great landholders and the larger urban-based entrepreneurs. His Krishak Praja Party (Peasants and Tenants Party) formed in 1929 drew up a platform of reform legislation to reduce rural indebtedness and foster peasant cooperatives; control rents and abolish landlords' customary exactions; and provide universal primary education "without taxation of the poor." A commission to review the land tenure system was also promised.

In 1935 five million new rural voters were enfranchised (three million of them Muslims, and 800,000 untouchables and tribals); they put the Krishak Praja Party into power to implement its proposals. That the Huq government's achievement did not match its pre-election rhetoric will come as little surprise, particularly when we note that Huq—a lawyer and tenure-holder from the Eastern Bengal district of Bakarganj—and all his influential party colleagues, were from that class of small-town notables who had so much invested in the existing system. A strengthening of the position of the rural middle-rung at the expense of the biggest men they would welcome, but fundamental change in the system they would not.

Depression, War, Famine, and Partition

Their radical talk, however, was heady stuff for a peasantry that had been exposed for a decade and a half, intermittently but at times intensively, to the propaganda of a procession of political activists: Gandhians, revolutionary terrorists, Muslim separatists, Hindu temple reformers and, most recently, Marxists. More importantly, that same peasantry was in the grip of a disastrous price recession.

From the beginning of the century, prices for Bengal's agricultural commodities had risen markedly, the main cash crop, jute, for example, selling in the mid-twenties for two-and-a-half to three times its 1900 price. In 1928 a 400-pound bale of raw jute was worth 74 rupees; by 1934 it could fetch scarcely 27. Short-term fluctuations in the price of a single commodity—fluctuations even this severe—were not unprecedented, but this slump lasted eight years and, with the depression worldwide, prices for all crops were affected.[9]

In the thirty years preceding the crash, rents had been steadily increased, and most peasants had attempted to convert their payments from produce to cash, in order to benefit from inflation. Now with rents fixed at a cash figure and prices tumbling, they were hoist with their own petard.[10] The Huq government tried to give relief by amortizing a portion of rural debts, but in many places this simply discouraged creditors from making new loans. Rural credit was nearly frozen, and the number of distress sales of holdings jumped dramatically. The chief beneficiaries were the middle-level tenure holders, who had the resources to retain their land, and in some cases add more from their distressed neighbors, but who were not under legislative attack as was the class above them.

For Bengal, as for most parts of India, the outbreak of World War II brought a sudden economic upturn. Agricultural prices, already recovering, shot to new levels; industry grew as never before, with an impact on mining and the transportation services. By 1942, however, with Burma in Japanese hands and large concentrations of British and American troops in and around Calcutta preparing to resist an invasion of eastern India, resource management in the region was clearly becoming too much for the skeleton British administration. Rice no longer came from Burma, Asia's greatest exporter in the interwar period, and the clearing of strategic areas of eastern Bengal as an anti-invasion tactic further reduced food supplies. The military were stockpiling, and, sensing an impending crisis, grain dealers began hoarding their supplies. The attempted "Quit India" revolution and a severe cyclone that devasted large areas of southwestern Bengal were the final straws. In 1943 famine gripped the region, killing between one and a half and two million people, of whom a majority died on the streets of Calcutta, whence they had dragged themselves in the vain hope of finding food. It was a hideous disaster, the more so because the fat cats in the countryside, who controlled what food grain there was, made a killing.[11]

Economic depression, war, and famine did not produce revolution in Bengal. They did aggravate the hostilities between religious communities, and these years were scarred with brutal communal rioting, which assumed the proportions of civil war for a time in 1946.

Why no peasant revolution? The answer clearly is that the conservative forces in the countryside had not been weakened in these years. Moreover, it was their political organizations, based in the rural towns, that were now devoted to communal confrontation.

The problems faced by radicals in this situation can be illustrated from the North Bengal district of Dinajpur, where the Kisan Sabha was taken over in 1938 by young Communists, part of the large body of Bengali terrorists whose long prison terms in the thirties had resulted in their conversion to Marxism. The appeals by these men to the peasantry provoked organized resistance from both the local Muslim League and the Kshatriya Samiti, the caste association of the dominant Rajbanshi community. Police repression ultimately drove them underground. It was not until late in 1946, with the upheavals accompanying the end of the war and the projected partition of Bengal, that they judged the time ripe for another revolutionary attempt. They launched the *Tebhaga* Movement: a demand that the *bhagadars* (sharecroppers) retain two-thirds instead of only one-half the crop. Their success in mobilizing peasant support for the agitation was unprecedented, but significantly much of that support came from tribals and ex-tribals[12] (the same communities, we should note, that were responsible for the Naxalbari movement twenty years later). Lack of support from the Muslims and caste Hindus insured the collapse of the agitation once sizable contingents of armed police were moved into the area. Within three months the Marxist leaders, almost all of whom were urban intellectuals, had been driven into hiding, and prominent peasant participants killed.[13]

Bengal was partitioned a few months later, two-thirds of its area (the rich eastern delta) going to Pakistan, and the drier, less fertile west, with Calcutta, remaining in India. In the former area the Muslim middle-peasants appear to have strengthened their hands at the expense of Hindu landlords and urban elites, most of whom were coerced into leaving for India by the early fifties. We know relatively little of the subsequent development of rural society in East Pakistan and Bangladesh, but it appears that there has been no radical redistribution of land.[14]

In West Bengal the Congress came to power after Independence committed to land redistribution, but in the first round—the *zamin-*

dari abolition legislation of 1954—and to a lesser extent in the second currently under way, fictitious transfers have protected all but the largest landlords from too serious a loss.[15] Even the communist parties—of which West Bengal has a number, all intractably opposed to one another—appear to have compromised with the local rural elites in their increasingly successful search for an electoral base in the countryside. Calcutta, full of dispossessed Eastern Bengal middle class, is a hotbed of radicalism, and there, in the coffee houses around the university, the peasantry of West Bengal and Bangladesh, indeed of the whole of Asia, are mobilized daily.

Mobilization Without Revolution

A central question is unresolved: why has there been no peasant revolution in this vast, depressed agricultural region? In the first place because there is no peasantry in the sense of a distinct rural class with a shared awareness of injustice suffered, or even of interests held in common. There are myriad divisions in Bengal rural society: local, regional, linguistic, religious, sectarian, racial, caste, tribal, class, and factional.[16] The strong binding ties are not horizontal—between those of similar occupation and economic status—but vertical—between kinsmen and caste fellows, often of widely divergent economic levels, and between clients and patrons. The conservative strength of these networks, to which we alluded earlier, lies in their ability to reward participants and effect reprisals against those who attempt to step out of line. We also noted the resistance of such a system to intrusions from the outside, unless (and the qualification is important) such intrusions are channeled through the networks, thereby reinforcing the power and prestige of the "bosses."

Such a system is not unique to Bengal and, on its own, is insufficient explanation of the absence of revolution. Other factors must be taken into account. One is the extensive penetration of the Bengal countryside through the past fifty years of formal political institutions, which have both reinforced the vertical patron-client-kin networks and hardened the lines of social division. Whether these are representative assemblies designed by government bureaucrats, such as the provincial and state legislatures, the municipalities, and the village councils, or political parties and interest groups constructed by politicians, their origin almost invariably has been Calcutta or one of the larger towns, and they have been linked to the countryside through the upper levels of the patron-client-kin networks.

Moreover, they have been organized in such a way as to reproduce the segmented character of rural society. Until at least the early fifties, voters for the representative councils, local as well as provincial, were organized into separate constituencies according to religion and race, caste and tribe. Similarly, the object of many of the voluntary associations was the representation of communal interests. This was the *raison d'être* of the caste and tribal associations, and of the Islamia Anjumans; there were political parties with the same avowed purpose.

The existence of these political institutions and the increasing degree of peasant participation in them, serves to remind us that peasant mobilization and peasant revolution are not synonymous. In Bengal, as elsewhere, peasants are often mobilized through institutions that serve to sustain, not threaten, the structures of power.

That those structures are oppressive for the vast majority of the peasantry in Bengal is a certainty. Why then are they tolerated? One answer has been suggested: to resist is to invite reprisals, and the cost of unsuccessful resistance is too high for most to contemplate seriously. Another answer is that not all peasants are equally oppressed. Indeed, as our discussion of the means by which power is acquired in rural Bengal should have indicated, it is often difficult to distinguish oppressed from the oppressor. Though every Bengal peasant has someone's boot on his neck, many have the concurrent satisfaction of stepping on someone else's face. Inequality, the bane of the hierarchical society, is also its chief delight.

Among those at the very bottom of the rural heap are the tribals, weak and vulnerable, but nursing a fierce sense of historic injury at the hands of caste Hindus and Muslims, who have stolen their land, shattered their tribal organization and their culture, exploited their labor, and dishonored their women. There is no risk of the tribals losing their sense of separate identity when they are constantly derided by the Hindus and Muslims as racial and cultural inferiors, and kept on the hungry margins of society. In their folk traditions they treasure memories of revolt, and the dead heroes of those uprisings are invested with messianic powers.[17] In their anger and despair the tribals are ready to revolt again, but there is no millenium in twentieth-century Bengal. The spectacle of these proud little men and women, led by urban intellectual radicals because they no longer have tribal leaders, pitting their bows and arrows against the rifles of the armed police, epitomizes the tragedy of rural Bengal.

1. Marcus F. Franda; *Radical Politics in West Bengal* (Cambridge, Mass., 1971), p. 173. On the Naxalites, see ibid., pp. 149–81, and Sankar Ghosh; "The Naxalite Struggle in West Bengal," *South Asian Review,* vol. 4, no. 2, Jan. 1971, pp. 99–105.

2. In 1911 only 6 percent of Bengal's population lived in towns, and of that urban population 41 percent was in Calcutta and Howrah. Seventy-five percent of the region's population was engaged in agriculture, and there were 600 people to the square mile *(Census of India, 1911).* Fifty years later 25 percent of the population of West Bengal (the Indian portion of partitioned Bengal) was urban, of which 88 percent was concentrated in the Calcutta metropolitan area. Fifty-four percent of the region's population was still employed in agriculture, and the population density had risen to 1,033 to the square mile *(Census of India, 1961).*

3. For a discussion of institutional politics in pre-Independence Bengal see J. H. Broomfield, *Elite Conflict in a Plural Society: Twentieth-Century Bengal* (Berkeley, 1968); and "The Social and Institutional Bases of Politics in Bengal, 1906–1947," *Aspects of Bengali History and Culture,* Rachel Baumer ed. (Honolulu, 1975); Leonard A. Gordon; *Bengal: the Nationalist Movement, 1876–1940* (New York, 1974); and John Gallagher; "Congress in Decline: Bengal, 1930–1939", *Modern Asian Studies,* vol. 7, part 3, July 1973, pp. 589–645.

4. See J. H. Broomfield, "The Rural Parvenu: a Report of Research in Progress", *South Asian Review,* vol. 6, no. 3, Apr. 1973, pp. 181–95.

5. It would be more accurate to say that Bengal had overlapping sets of land-tenure systems. As a consequence, the names for similar tenures varied from one locality to the next. The elaborate subinfeudation was the source of interminable disputes over land rights, and the resulting judicial cases impoverished many a landed family, while enriching their lawyers. (See Tapan Raychaudhuri, "Permanent Settlement in Operation, Bakarganj District, East Bengal," *Land Control and Social Structure in Indian History,* Robert Eric Frykenberg, ed. (Madison, 1969), pp. 163–74; and *Report of the Land Revenue Commission, Bengal* (Alipore, 1940).

6. J. A. Pitt-Rivers, *The People of the Sierra* (London, 1954), p. 140.

7. See Broomfield, *Elite Conflict,* pp. 210–12, 224–26.

8. For a general discussion of caste associations, see Lloyd I. and Susanne Hoeber Rudolph, *The Modernity of Tradition: Political Development in India* (Chicago, 1967), pp. 17–154; R.S. Khare; *The Changing Brahmans: Associations and Elites Among the Kanya-Kubjas of North India* (Chicago, 1970), pp. 195–221; and Imtiaz Ahmad; "Caste Mobility Movements in North India," *Indian Economic and Social History Review,* vol. 8, no. 2, June 1971, pp. 164–91.

9. Dharm Narain, *The Impact of Price Movements on Areas Under Selected Crops in India, 1900–1939* (Cambridge, 1965), pp. 163–66.

10. Binay Bhusan Chaudhuri; "Agrarian Movements in Bengal and Bihar, 1919–1939," *Socialism in India,* B. R. Nanda, ed. (Delhi, n.d.), p. 202; *Report of the Bengal Provincial Banking Enquiry Committee, 1929–30* (Calcutta, 1930); and N. C. Bhattacharyya & L.A. Natesan, eds., *Some Bengal Villages. An Economic Survey* (Calcutta, 1932).

11. *Famine Enquiry Commission: Report on Bengal* (New Delhi, 1945).

12. The term "ex-tribal" has been applied by anthropologists to those who have attempted to become Hindus through the adaptation of their group culture to what they perceive to be Hindu mores, but whose tribal antecedents are still evident to the caste Hindus and Muslims among whom they live.

13. Sunil Sen, *Agrarian Struggle in Bengal, 1946–47* (New Delhi, 1972); and Hamza Alavi, "Peasants and Revolution," *Socialist Register 1965,* Ralph Miliband and John Savile, eds. (London, 1965), pp. 265–77.

14. The only case studies of rural Eastern Bengal since the 1947 partition have been produced by scholars associated with the Pakistan Academy for Rural Development at Comilla. They deal with the area encompassed by the Academy's development program, and as such are probably unrepresentative. As examples see Mary Jane Beech et al., *Inside the East Pakistan Village—Six Articles* (East Lansing, 1966); and S.M. Hafeez Zaidi, *The Village Culture in Transition: A Study of East Pakistan Rural Society* (Honolulu, 1970). For more general material see Azizur Rahman Khan, *The Economy of Bangladesh* (London, 1972), and "Bangladesh: Economic Policies Since Independence," *South Asian Review,* vol. 8, no. 1, Oct. 1974, pp. 13–32.

15. During the symposium, I commented upon the consistency with which peasantries have been betrayed with promises of land redistribution. A pattern is clearly discernible: politicians seeking to mobilize a peasantry in order to gain power promise land redistribution; once in power they redistribute land in such a way as to gain or retain the support of powerful sections of rural society. The weak are calculatingly excluded.

16. For an excellent case study illustrating this see Ralph W. Nicholas, "Village Factions and Political Parties in Rural West Bengal," *Journal of Commonwealth Political Studies,* vol. 2, no. 1, Nov. 1963, pp. 17–32.

17. See for example Suresh Singh; *The Dust-Storm and the Hanging Mist: a Study of Birsa Munda and His Movement in Chotanagpur, 1874–1901* (Calcutta, 1966).

Peasants in the Mexican Revolution of 1910

FRIEDRICH KATZ

ONE OF THE MOST POWERFUL SOCIAL UPHEAVALS THAT HAS taken place on the American continent in this century is the Mexican Revolution of 1910. It is generally held to be of agrarian character, for the majority of its participants were peasants, and it resulted in some of the most advanced agrarian legislation in America. The Agrarian Law of January 1915, drafted by the Carranza government, and the constitution of 1917 seem to testify to that fact. They establish, among other things, the return of lands to village communities that had been deprived of them by the large estates, the redistribution of a large part of these estates to landless peasants, and the expropriation of foreign-held lands.[1]

Nevertheless, the Mexican Revolution was very different from other social revolutions in which the peasantry was involved. In France, four years after the outbreak of the Revolution of 1789, most of the large estates had been destroyed. In Russia this process was even more rapid. When, immediately after taking power, Lenin and the Bolsheviks issued their decree on expropriation of large estates, they were, to a large extent, ratifying a process that was going on all over Russia.

In Mexico the large-scale redistribution of lands began in 1934, more than twenty years after the outbreak of the revolution. Great revolutionary upheavals, the nearly complete destruction of the prerevolutionary army and state administration between 1910 and 1920 did not lead to substantial agrarian reforms. Only 167,936 hectares of land were distributed to 46,398 peasants during this period. From 1934 to 1940, after a peaceful transition from the presidency of Rodriguez to that of Cardenas, 811,157 peasants obtained 17,906,429 hectares of land.[2] What is the explanation for these patterns of development that make the Mexican Revolution so different from other social upheavals? It is in this context that I would like to examine peasant movements in Mexico, their relations to other groups of society and the emergence of peasant organizations.

The Mexican Peasantry

Prior to the revolution the Mexican peasantry was divided into four large groups: free villages, tribal communities on the frontier, hacienda residents, and small landowners (rancheros).

Free villages had managed to retain a large part of their communal lands throughout the Aztec, Spanish colonial, and early Mexican independence period, although the Aztec, Spanish, and Mexican governments had allowed and sometimes encouraged the transfer of part of the communally held lands to large property owners. The term "free" only meant that these villages had succeeded in keeping a certain degree of political and economic independence, which was always limited in nature. While they maintained their traditional village authorities, they were dependent both politically and economically on the state and on the neighboring haciendas. All villages had to pay tribute to the state, sometimes in products, sometimes in labor. Many of their inhabitants also worked for neighboring haciendas. In the sixteenth and seventeenth centuries, this type of labor was largely coercive (induced by such institutions as the Repartimiento and Encomienda). By the late seventeenth and early eighteenth century, loss of village lands coupled with an increase in population created mainly economic causes for part-time work on haciendas. Nevertheless, until the 1870s for most of these communities the village lands provided their basic subsistence, while income from work on haciendas was a supplement, though a necessary one.[3]

The advent of the dictatorship of Porfirio Díaz with its large-scale expropriation of communal lands reversed this tendency. In 1910, between eighty and ninety percent of all Mexican peasants were practically landless. Income from work on the haciendas had become their main source of revenue, while the proceeds from village lands, if they existed at all, constituted only a small supplement. Nevertheless, most of the residential areas of the villages still belonged to them, and the communities had retained their traditional social organizations. The relationships between these villages and the haciendas were extremely varied. In maize- and wheat-producing areas, many villagers worked as tenants on hacienda lands. On plantations producing crops such as sugar, coffee, and tobacco, they tended to be employed as temporary laborers during the planting and harvest season.[4]

Sometimes they worked on the haciendas that had expropriated their lands. Generally, the hacendados preferred to employ laborers from more remote regions, with whom they had had no direct conflicts.[5]

In some ways similar and in many ways quite different from the communal villages, the tribal communities were essentially a product of the Mexican frontier. In the seventeenth and eighteenth centuries religious orders (mainly the Jesuits and Franciscans) had set up missions among those Indian tribes that the Spaniards had never managed to conquer. These missions were essentially theocratic states based on the principle of indirect rule.

In return for accepting the political, religious, and economic domination of the missionaries, the tribal communities of the north were allowed to retain all their lands. Unlike the free Indian villages in central Mexico, the northern communities kept their tribal organizations. In some cases, as in that of the Yaquis of Sonora, the missionaries even created tribal authorities where none had existed before. This meant the maintenance of a large Indian aristocracy closely allied to the missionaries. Unlike the villages of central Mexico, many of these communities were even allowed to retain their arms.

While in central Mexico the technical changes brought in by the Spaniards had contradictory effects (Aztec irrigation works were neglected, Spanish livestock overran Indian fields, etc.), in some parts of the north innovations were more beneficial to the Indians. The introduction of livestock, the plow, and irrigation in the arid lands of the north greatly increased the resources at the disposal of the Indian tribes.[6]

These factors explain the passivity with which some warlike northern tribes acceded to missionary control and the profound influence

63

that religious orders were able to exert on them long after Spanish colonial rule ended.[7]

After the achievement of independence, Mexican authorities made large-scale efforts to confiscate the lands of these tribal groups. By the end of the nineteenth century their efforts were, to a large degree, successful.

One of the most important segments of the prerevolutionary Mexican peasantry were the resident peons on haciendas, sometimes called *gañanes* or *naboríos* and sometimes peones *acasillados*. They comprised three main groups. The first was composed of tenants and sharecroppers; while their main work consisted in tending the land rented or parceled out to them by the hacienda, they were required to work demesne lands during part of the year. A second group of laborers mainly worked demesne lands and only in their spare time tended to small plots put at their disposal by the hacienda, the proceeds of which were used for their subsistence. Cowboys and shepherds constituted the third group of permanent hacienda inhabitants.

Many of these resident workers were tied to the hacienda by such coercive measures as debt peonage. This institution was most developed in Mexico's southeast, where labor was scarce; by the beginning of the twentieth century it was weakest in northern Mexico, where American ranches and American and Mexican mines competed for hacienda labor.[8]

In contrast to the communal villages and the tribal communities, the small rancheros constituted the only group of small landowners who were on the increase during the nineteenth and early twentieth century. Unlike these other two groups of peasants, the small rancheros were extremely heterogeneous both in their origins and their development.

Some of them constituted a heritage of the colonial period. A few were the descendants of Spanish foot soldiers who had received small plots of land after the conquest of Mexico in the sixteenth century. Many more were descended from military colonists who had been granted land in the northern frontier region of New Spain in the latter part of the eighteenth century in order to ward off the attacks of marauding Indian tribes.

This was the origin of the villages and towns of Casas Grandes, Galeana, Namiquipa, Janos, and Cruces. In 1778 the Spanish governor of the province of Nueva Vizcaya (the present state of Chihuahua), offered inhabitants of the province of whatever "caste, class or social status" lands, water, a subsidy of two reales a day for one year, and exemption from taxes for ten years if they settled in one of these colonies. They would have to remain there for at least ten years and fight nomadic Indians wherever called upon to do so. They would not be allowed to divide their holdings but, unlike the inhabitants of the free Indian villages, they were permitted to sell them. The colonies were considered independent municipalities and enjoyed a wide margin of self-government.[9]

The majority of the small rancheros constituted a relatively new group that had developed to a large degree in the nineteenth century. Many were better-off members of village communities who, when the village was expropriated, had managed to retain their lands, to buy land from the hacienda or to acquire confiscated church lands. Some were wealthy tenants, while others were returning emigrants from the United States who had invested their savings in small ranches.

Throughout the nineteenth century two of these four groups of peasants, the free Indian villagers and the northern tribes, had fought the hacendados and the Mexican government in order to retain their lands.

The free villages had staged local uprisings, appealed to the courts, or tried to form political alliances with contending factions in Mexico. In the first half of the nineteenth century, as long as the central government was weak and the economic incentives for expropriation (due to a lack of markets) were not too strong, they met with some measure of success. The establishment of a strong centralized national administration in the Porfirian era, the rapid economic expansion due to foreign investment, the building of railroads,[10] and the appearance of new markets gave the hacendados and politicians the motivation and strength to expropriate communal village lands and crush peasant resistance.

The rising of the northern tribal communities were militarily far more effective than the isolated struggles of central Mexican villages, but by the beginning of the twentieth century, the most tenacious of these tribes, the Yaquis of Sonora, had been greatly weakened, though not defeated.[11]

In contrast to these two groups, the resident hacienda peons not only tended to be passive, but frequently fought for the hacienda. In the great rising of free Maya villages against the hacendados and the Mexican authorities in the mid-nineteenth century, many of the Maya peons on the haciendas sided with the estate owners against the village communities.[12]

The Revolution of 1910, which began as a political rebellion against Porfirian autocracy by liberal hacendados and part of the Mexican middle classes, led to a number of peasant uprisings.

In the three largest such revolts, three of the four peasant groups participated. The one sector of the peasantry that was conspicuously absent in this first phase of the Mexican Revolution were the *acasillados*.

The Zapata Revolt in Morelos

The best known of the peasant revolutionary movements in the first phase of the Mexican Revolution was the Zapata revolt in the state of Morelos. So much has been written about the Zapatistas that there is little need to elaborate. It was essentially a revolt of communal villagers whose lands had been expropriated by neighboring sugar haciendas. Such expropriations had taken place all over central Mexico, although they may have been of unusual intensity in Morelos. This intensity alone does not account for the fact that this state became the center of agrarian revolt in Mexico. Morelos had a number of factors that greatly favored the outbreak of revolutionary movements: impenetrable mountains, the proximity of Mexico City (which made access to new ideas, information, and arms much easier than elsewhere in central Mexico), a great density of population, a tradition of political struggle for the governorship, which shortly before had united villages whose relations with each other had been extremely limited until then. The revolt was directed by leaders elected according to ancient traditions by the village communities.[13]

The Yaqui Indians in Sonora

The second focus of revolt was the northwestern state of Sonora, where the Yaqui Indians revolted once more. While their immediate leaders were tribal chieftains, they had subordinated their movement to Mexican "patrons," who were far from being peasants.

The politician whose influence was greatest among the Yaquis was the leader of the Maderista party in Sonora and one of the richest hacendados in the state, José María Maytorena. At least in the political field, Maytorena was in no way a reformer such as Madero tried to be, but simply an out "who" wanted to "in." He had become a patron for the Yaquis, since he was willing to employ fugitive Yaqui rebels as laborers on his haciendas and to protect them from government persecution. Not having been granted lands taken from the Yaquis by the state government, he had never incurred the Indians' animosity.[14]

De la Huerta, who for many years had been one of Maytorena's hacienda managers and had carried out this policy, was also recognized as a patron by the Yaquis.[15]

The Revolutionary Movement in Chihuahua

The preceding pattern of peasants' subordinating their movements to a nonpeasant leadership was characteristic of most revolutionary movements in Mexico with the exception of Morelos.

It was certainly the case for the revolutionary movement that was most effective in toppling the Díaz dictatorship: the rising of small rancheros in the northern state of Chihuahua.

These rancheros constituted an atypical and in many senses unique social group in Mexico. They were descendants of military colonists who had received land and economic support first from the Spanish colonial administration and later from the Mexican government in return for fighting against nomadic Indian tribes from the north, especially against the Apaches.

They had fought uninterruptedly until 1885 when the Apaches were decisively defeated. During this period they had acquired military skills, arms as well as the consciousness of constituting a special elite fighting against the "barbarians." In 1908, in a letter to the president of the republic, the inhabitants of one of these colonies, Namiquipa, wrote: "because of constant attacks by the savages all neighboring haciendas . . . were abandoned between 1832 and 1860; only Namiquipa continued to fight and constituted a bulwark of civilization in this far-off region."[16]

During the Indian wars these colonists had enjoyed the economic and military support of the state government as well as that of the wealthiest hacendados, such as the Terrazas family, together with whom they had fought the Apaches.

With the defeat of the Indian tribes, the attitude of the hacendados toward the military colonists began to change. On the one hand the colonists were no longer needed to ward off Apache raids; on the other hand their lands were becoming increasingly attractive to Chihuahua's great landowners. Land values along the route of the Mexican Central Railway, which crossed Chihuahua from north to south, and the Chihuahua Pacific Railway, which passed through the western part of the state, rose sharply. The same was true of lands located near the border of the United States whose value was increased by the economic development of the American Southwest. Most of the military colonies had been established in these regions and from 1900 onward Chihuahua's hacendados, at first with the tacit approval and after 1904 with the enthusiastic support of the state government, did everything in their power to expropriate the lands of these colonies. In 1903 Toribio Ortega, who headed the "Junta directiva de los Vecinos de Cuchillo Parado," a military colony that had been granted land by Benito Juarez in 1865, protested in the name of 834 inhabitants against a planned attack on their rights by a neighboring hacendado. "We know"—he stated in a telegram to the Federal Ministry of Development—"that Licenciado Carlos Muñoz is trying to obtain 10 sitios de ganado mayor belonging to the Colony of Cuchillo Parado. Since the documents he has in his possession were obtained by force, we ask you to discard his claims."[17]

Cuchillo Parado succeeded in warding off the attack, but the situation of the military colonies greatly worsened after Chihuahua's largest landowning family, the Terrazas-Creel clan, assumed the governorship of the state in 1903.[18] In 1905 a special law was passed

68

by the state legislature of Chihuahua that facilitated the expropriation of the military colonies. By 1908 some of the oldest and most prestigious of these colonies began to feel the effects of these measures. "We are deeply concerned about the fact that lands we consider our own, since we have received them from our fathers and worked them with our hands, are now passing into other hands," the inhabitants of Namiquipa wrote President Porfirio Díaz in 1908, ". . . if you do not grant us your protection, we will have to abandon our homes in order to subsist."[19]

An emissary sent to Mexico City to represent the population of another of Chihuahua's oldest military colonies, Janos, bitterly complained to President Díaz "The owners of the colony of Fernandez Leal located two leagues from Janos are enjoying a comfortable life in the United States while we, who suffered from the invasions of barbarians whom our fathers fought, cannot keep our own lands."[20]

Other former military colonies had a similar fate. Appeals to the national government for help were fruitless, and it is not surprising that these colonists played a key role in the Revolution of 1910. Toribio Ortega, who had led the inhabitants of Cuchillo Parado in their struggle against the hacendados in 1903, was the first revolutionary leader to rise against Porfirio Díaz in 1910. He later became one of Pancho Villa's most trusted generals.[21] Porfirio Talamantes, the spokesman for Janos, also participated in the Revolution and became a colonel in Villa's army.[22] The village of Namiquipa was a center of revolutionary activity in Chihuahua from 1910 to 1920. When Pancho Villa attacked Columbus, New Mexico, in 1916, a large part of his striking force was composed of inhabitants of Namiquipa.[23]

Had the Revolution in Chihuahua been limited to the expropriated military colonists, their fighting capacity and arms would already have constituted a formidable challenge to the Mexican government. Since these people were by no means isolated, but united with other groups of rural and urban society in Chihuahua, their movement gained decisive importance for the course of Revolution in Mexico.

In 1910 they were joined by two other sectors of the rural population: many of the rancheros who had managed to retain their lands and a sector of the rural population that was rapidly increasing in

Chihuahua, semi-agricultural and semi-industrial laborers. The latter worked part of the year as sharecroppers or agricultural workers on haciendas and spent the rest of the time as mine laborers, lumbermen, or migrant workers in the United States.

The region with the largest concentration of small landowners as well as agrarian-industrial workers was the district of Guerrero, in the mountainous region of the Sierra Madre in Chihuahua.

From 1908 onward they were hit by a number of natural and economic catastrophes that grew worse from year to year. From 1904 to 1907, a large part of the corn production in Chihuahua shifted from the irrigated lands of the Camargo district to the nonirrigated soils of Guerrero.[24]

The lands of Guerrero were subject to extremely insecure weather conditions, and the harvests of 1908–1910 were poor. Bad harvests were not new in Guerrero, but they had never been as catastrophic as in those three years. Increasing demand for corn on the one hand and government sale of good public lands on the other had led to increasing use of marginal soils that were greatly affected by the crop failure. In other times the peasants had been able to find work in neighboring mines, or even in the United States, and to obtain credit from the state's banks to tide them over. But from 1907 to 1910, Mexico was greatly affected by a recession in the United States. Mines closed down, many Mexican laborers were dismissed by American companies in the southwestern United States, and banks in Chihuahua did not grant credit.[25] The state government not only refused to do anything for the peasants, but forced them to pay increasing taxes while the large haciendas paid practically nothing. Since political power in Chihuahua, control of the largest bank in the state, of its main haciendas, and some of its mines were concentrated in the hands of one family, the Terrazas-Creel clan, this family soon became the focus of all resentment and bitterness in the state.[26]

The men who led the Guerrero movement, which became the focus of the Revolution in Chihuahua, were not peasants themselves but, with one exception, members of the district's traditional elite. Abraham Gonzalez, who directed the revolutionary movement in Chihuahua, belonged to a family that for a long time had dominated the political and economic life of the Guerrero district and had played an important role in Chihuahua politics. By the beginning of the twentieth century, the family had gradually been displaced by the Terrazas-Creel clan, and Gonzalez had had to make a living successively as a rancher, an accountant for a streetcar company, a translator, and a cattle salesman.[27]

Pascual Orozco, the military leader of the revolt, came from a well-known family in the district. He was not a peasant but a muleteer.[28]

The one conspicuous exception to this rule was Pancho Villa, who came from the state of Durango and had originally been a sharecropper. When the Revolution broke out, Villa alternated between being one of the state's best-known social bandits and working as a cattle dealer—two professions that were not in absolute contradiction.[29] Apart from the fact that the monopoly of political and economic power exercised by the Terrazas clan in Chihuahua had managed to unite the most divergent social groups in the state, the success of the revolutionaries was due to two other factors. The border with the United States provided easy access to arms. The middle-class composition of a large part of the revolutionary forces made it easier for them than for the Zapatistas in Morelos or the Yaquis in Sonora to gain the support of the urban population.

It was the Chihuahua revolutionaries who were mainly instrumental in forcing Porfirio Díaz to resign. His successor, Madero, who became president in 1911, shared the fate of many of the moderate leaders in the first phase of a social revolution. Wishing to limit the Revolution basically to political changes, he soon lost the support of the most radical of his original adherents, mainly large sectors of the peasantry, while the conservatives continued to oppose him. In February 1913 he was toppled by an army coup and murdered.

In most revolutions such coups or attempted coups by the right generated sharp reactions by the left, which mobilized large groups of the peasantry by carrying out radical agrarian reforms. The attempt of Louis XVI to flee France in 1790 played an important role in the Jacobin assumption of power and in the radical dissolution of the landed estates of the French nobility. In Russia the Kornilov putsch led to the October Revolution and to the land distribution measures of the Bolsheviks. In China, after the massacre of the urban communists in Shanghai in 1927 by Chiang Kai-shek, the remnants of the Communist Party moved into rural Kiangsi province, where they carried out land reforms and organized an essentially peasant army.[30]

Northern Revolutionaries and Agrarian Reforms

The Mexican case was radically different from that of France, Russia, or China. The main body of Mexican revolutionaries in the north managed to mobilize a large army of peasants practically without carrying out any large-scale agrarian reforms and by limiting themselves to radical promises and programs. Instead of paying the peasant soldiers with social reforms as the French, Russian, and Chinese revolutionaries, as well as the Zapatistas in southern Mexico, did, they paid them in cash. Their alliance with the United States permitted them to do so.

The motives for this alliance are extremely complex and would go far beyond the scope of this paper. While Woodrow Wilson and William Jennings Bryan may partially have been motivated by their progressive ideology in helping the Mexican revolutionaries,[31] this was certainly not the case for the large business interests who cooperated with northern Mexican forces.

In return for paying large taxes to the "constitucionalistas," Doheny's Mexican petroleum company and large mining interests hoped not only to buy immunity from confiscations, depredations, and strikes, but also to secure low-cost lands and properties held by Mexican hacendados and European investors, as well as to obtain concessions from the revolutionary government.[32] They were not entirely unsuccessful, since American investments in Mexico increased in the revolutionary period.[33]

This alliance affected the agrarian policy of the northern revolutionary movement in at least five different ways:

1. The most obvious effect was that foreign-owned estates controlling one-seventh of all lands in Mexico were not touched by the revolutionaries.

2. Conservative politicians opposed to agrarian reforms who had played an important role in the first phase of the Mexican Revolution

could continue to do so without changing their agrarian policies. Thanks to taxes and contributions paid by American companies, American arms and the revenue from the sale of Mexican goods to the United States (which could only take place with the tacit approval of the administration in Washington), Carranza managed to set up a large army composed primarily of peasants. He could do this without granting significant amounts of land to the peasantry and he was able to limit himself to plans and promises he never kept.

When Huerta's military coup took place, the Maderista governor of Sonora, Maytorena, left the country. He had feared that the only way to carry out a revolution was through "a general confiscation of property."[34] He was a liberal but, above all, he was a class-conscious hacendado and confiscating the holdings of his peers (and perhaps finally losing his own property in the process) was something he could not abide. When he became convinced that it would be possible to finance the Revolution without large-scale agrarian changes, he returned to Sonora to assume the leadership of the state's revolutionary movement. Both he and Carranza did everything in their power to prevent agrarian reforms from being implemented in the territories they controlled. When General Cabral, another Sonoran revolutionary, proposed an agrarian law, the "revolutionary" state parliament had no compunctions about rejecting it.[35] Carranza harshly rebuked a subordinate of his, General Lucio Blanco, who had begun to distribute the lands of a large hacienda among peasants.[36]

3. Even radical revolutionaries who favored large-scale land distribution, such as Pancho Villa, who had confiscated all large Mexican-owned haciendas in the state of Chihuahua, were persuaded not to carry out their plans. Faced with the choice of dividing up the haciendas among the peasantry or having them at least provisionally administered by the state, Villa chose the latter course. State administration of the haciendas assured him large revenues that he could use to finance the buying of arms and supplies in the United States.

The state's administrators were his own generals, many of whom began to consider these estates as their property and sharply opposed any agrarian reform. This new "bourgeoisie" and the Villistás increased need for American supplies became significant obstacles to any large-scale agrarian reform in the territories controlled by Pancho Villa.[37]

4. The "professional" armies originally composed of peasants that emerged from the northern Revolution later had no compunctions about putting down peasant uprisings that their military leaders did not want.[38]

5. No peasant organizations of any kind were established in northern Mexico until 1920. No effective elections for municipal or state government were carried out between 1913 and 1920. Power rested in the hands of the revolutionary army, which became more and more distant and alienated from the civilian population.

Southern Revolutionaries and Agrarian Reforms

The situation was entirely different in the southern part of Mexico where Zapata's revolutionary forces were in control. There agrarian commissions were set up who returned expropriated lands to communal villages. A civilian administration in which the traditional village communities played a decisive role was elected.[39] While conflicts between the military and the civilians arose, the army's dependence on peasant support assured a large measure of civilian control.

It would, nevertheless, be too simple to attribute the different roles of the peasantry in northern and southern Mexico and the implementation of agrarian reform in the south exclusively to the funds and the arms the northern revolutionaries received from the United States.

Peasants constituted a smaller part of the total population of the north than of that of the south. While over eighty percent of the population of the state of Morelos was peasant, this was true for only about forty percent of Chihuahua's working population. The rest of the state's labor force was composed of cowboys and nonagricultural workers. In the south the peasantry consisted mainly of free villagers; while in the north it was made up to a much larger degree of hacienda peons. The free villagers had a century-old organization capable of mobilizing them and a clear-cut aim for which to fight: the restoration of traditional village lands and rights. The hacienda peons had neither. This may explain why there are practically no instances in Mexican history of spontaneous rising by hacienda peons.

Apart from these resident peons, another important rural group in northern Mexico consisted of cowboys, whose interest in agrarian reform was limited. The importance of these two groups in the northern countryside, as well as the fact that some of the most revolutionary peasants were in the army far from their native villages, may explain why no jacqueries, no spontaneous land seizures, occurred in northern Mexico.[40]

Split Between the Conservative and Radical Revolutionaries

The fact that it was from these two groups that the haciendas had always picked their most trusted retainers furnishes an additional explanation why they had no compunctions about fighting against the most radical groups in the Revolution when the split between conservatives and radicals took place in 1914.

This split did not and does not seem as clear-cut as in other revolutions. Regional divisions not always linked to social divisions were important. The official programs of both groups as well as their foreign policy were similar to a large degree. As far as labor was concerned, the generally more conservative Carranza faction managed to make more promises and gain more support than their far more parochial and peasant-oriented rivals of the Villa-Zapata faction. Nevertheless, one basic issue divided the more conservative Carranza group from the Zapatistas and Villistas: whether to keep or to return the confiscated lands of the haciendas. Both Zapata, who had divided the haciendas among the peasants, and Villa, who had not but was contemplating such a division, were sharply opposed to any kind of return of the confiscated estates to their confiscated estates to the hacendados.[42]

With the help of the estate owners who rallied to his cause, as well as with the support of the American government, Carranza managed to defeat the radical wing of the revolutionaries.

After their victory, the triumphant moderates could, nevertheless, not return to the policies of the prerevolutionary Díaz government. The years of fighting as well as the radical programs drafted by

75

Carranza and his supporters had aroused large-scale expectations among the peasantry. They could not be entirely ignored.

While Carranza had cooperated closely with the United States in the first phase of the Revolution, cooperation was becoming more and more difficult for him after his victory. On the one hand, he was forced to respond to ever-increasing nationalistic pressures brought about by the Revolution. On the other hand, as the country's economy declined, Carranza's main source of revenue were taxes imposed on American oil and mining companies, and also on sisal being sold to the United States.

As relations with the United States became more strained, the government found that its possibility of controlling the huge armies that had arisen during the Revolution became more and more limited. It did not have the funds to pay for all of them, and regional caudillos began to control parts of Mexico independently of the federal government. At the same time the hacendados who had recovered their lands began to arm retainers and pose a serious challenge for the government.

Therefore the government was more and more forced to set up popular organizations to counter these threats. Its policies in the 1916–1928 period bear striking resemblances to that of the Directoire in the post-Jacobin era of the French Revolution. In the same way as the Directoire, the Mexican government was trying to play off the left and the right against each other. When pressures from the United States, from dissident army groups, and from the hacendados became too strong, it began mobilizing popular support and carrying out some reforms. When the popular organizations got out of hand, it called back the army and the hacendados to fight them. This policy made it necessary for the government to set up peasant organizations but at the same time to firmly control them.

The first such peasant organization that the government established was in a region where the danger, both from the hacendados and the United States, was great, a region where peasant organizations could help the government obtain revenues and where it could mobilize the peasantry and gain their support without carrying out large-scale land reform. Such a situation existed in the state of Yucatán, in southeastern Mexico.

Government Attempts to Organize the Peasantry

In 1915 the hacendados of Yucatán, together with the Chicago-based International Harvester Corporation, which was the main buyer for Yucatán sisal, had sponsored a military uprising in Yucatán. In that same year the Sonoran General Salvador Alvarado landed in Yucatán with a Carranzista army and put down the rebellion. Yucatán was very important to the Mexican government. Due to World War I, which prevented the importation of East African sisal to the United States, the price of Yucatán sisal had sharply increased on United States markets. Alvarado set up a government buying and selling monopoly, the Compania Reguladora del Mercado del Henequen. This monopoly bought sisal at relatively low prices from the hacendados and sold it at high prices to the International Harvester Corporation. The difference went to finance the central government in Mexico City as well as Alvarado and his army. It is obvious that this policy did not arouse great enthusiasm either among the hacendados or the International Harvester Corporation. The latter was strongly pressuring the American government to intervene in Yucatán, something Wilson would not do. Nevertheless, it was obvious to Alvarado that without popular support, it would be difficult to maintain control of the Yucatán Peninsula. From 1916 onward he began organizing peasant unions on all large haciendas in the state. These unions secured substantial advantages for the peasantry short of agrarian reform. Debt peonage, which had been prevalent on all Yucatán haciendas was abolished, while part of the revenues from the increasing price of sisal was used to increase wages paid to hacienda laborers. The result was that Alvarado had managed to gain a large measure of popular support without confiscating the haciendas.[43]

This tactic was only applicable in regions where large incomes from sales of crops to the United States as well as the existence of debt peonage made it possible to win over the peasantry without, at least at first, giving them lands. In central Mexico, such a tactic would have had no success. There the clear-cut demand of the village communities was for the return of their lands. During Carranza's term in office until 1920 no serious efforts were made to organize the peasantry outside of Yucatán, since Carranza was firmly opposed to

77

any large-scale agrarian reform. This situation changed in 1920 when a group of military men under the leadership of Obregón took power in Mexico. Unlike Carranza, who had been an hacendado, Obregón had originally been a small rancher and had more radical agrarian ideas. But above all, the threat from the United States had greatly increased. World War I had ended, and the Americans now had a free hand to intervene in Mexico if they wished to do so. Woodrow Wilson's term in office was ending, and chances were good that a president much more inclined to intervention in Mexico than Wilson would take office. The increasing opposition of the United States also encouraged increasing risings by dissatisfied military caudillos as well as by rebellious hacendados. The Obregón government reacted by trying to increase its basis of popular support.

On the one hand the government encouraged the formation of labor unions and even armed its members. On the other hand it made its peace with the Zapatistas who were still fighting by granting them the lands they had taken. It also made an agreement with Pancho Villa, who obtained a large hacienda for himself and his soldiers. At the same time the government tolerated and frequently encouraged the organization of agrarian parties and peasant unions in very different regions of Mexico. In return for supporting the government, both electorally and with arms, the members of these unions were granted lands. From 1920 to 1924 the amount of land given to peasants increased greatly in contrast to the period between 1917 and 1920.

While it needed their support, the government never allowed these peasant unions to get out of hand, which means it never allowed them to obtain a large measure of political autonomy.

If the peasant unions tried to do so, the government clamped down on such organizations or withdrew its support of them. Frequently this meant the end of the peasant organizations. Sometimes it led to the creation of autonomous unions, really independent of the government. This happened in Yucatán after Alvarado left and a more radical leader, Felipe Carrillo Puerto, took over. As the price of sisal fell after the end of World War I, the peasant unions demanded the division of the hacienda lands. When the government withdrew its support because the unions were going too far, Carrillo Puerto created his own organization, the Partido Socialista del Sureste. In

Veracruz and in the cotton-producing Laguna area of northern Mexico, the peasant unions that had lost the support of the government established links with the slowly emerging Communist Party of Mexico.[44] In spite of these offshoots, the government on the whole could count on the support of peasant organizations up to 1928. When it faced the opposition of either the military, the United States, or the Church, the agraristas would take up arms in favor of the government.[45]

In 1928 Obregón's successor, Calles, made his peace with the United States and the Church and clearly indicated that, in his opinion, agrarian reform had gone too far. The peasant unions lost government support and, in many cases, their leaders were killed or driven into exile. The result was that part of the peasant organizations disappeared, while an important segment joined different radical groups, mainly the Communist Party. As the Great Depression of 1929 began to affect Mexico more and more, these groups, together with labor organizations who had suffered the same fate at the hands of Calles, began to form a significant opposition to the Mexican government.

It was this pressure, as well as the emergence of the most nationalistic government Mexico ever produced, the Cardenas administration, which could not implement its policies without a large degree of popular support, that led to an entirely new agrarian policy.

The government carried out the most extensive agrarian reform in Mexico's history. From 1934 to 1940, 17,906,429 hectares of land were distributed to 811,157 peasants. At the same time, the peasant organizations were placed under the firm control of Mexico's ruling party, the Partido de la Revolución Mexicana.

Summary

The Mexican Revolution of 1910 produced two types of movements in which peasants participated:

1. The Zapatista movement in central Mexico consisting mainly of expropriated communal villagers whose basic aim was the restoration of their lost lands. This movement was led by peasants mostly elected according to the established traditions of their communities.

The Zapatistas confiscated the lands of the large estates and returned most of them to the villages that had originally owned them.

2. A series of northern revolutionary movements composed of hacienda peons, cowboys, small rancheros, and industrial workers, with practically no peasants among their main leaders, with the exception of a few men such as Obregon or Calles, who had been rancheros for a time. The social origin of these leaders ranged from liberal hacendados to members of the upper and lower middle class and some men who could be defined as social bandits. Largely due to American help and to the proximity of the American border, the more conservative among these northern movements could defeat both the federal army, supported by Mexico's traditional oligarchy, and the Zapatista movement of central Mexico. The liberal hacendados produced a substantial amount of radical rhetoric never matched by practical applications, with the notable exception of the abolition of debt peonage.

Peasant organizations, consisting mainly of hacienda peons, emerged only in a small part of the country between 1915 and 1920 when the liberal hacendados were in power. Practically no land reform was carried out from 1915 to 1920, with only 46,398 peasant receiving 167,936 hectares of land.

The overthrow of the liberal hacendado leadership of Mexico by a rising middle class facing an increasing number of external and internal opponents led to attempts to create an alliance with at least part of the communal villagers of central Mexico. The Zapatista revolutionaries were not only granted amnesty, but also the possession of the lands they had seized. In return, the Zapatista leaders participated in the organization and development of the Partido Nacional Agrarista, which was closely linked to the Obregón government and which tried to mobilize the peasantry of central Mexico to support the administration. To secure peasant support, the Mexican government increased the rate of agrarian redistribution far above the level of the previous administration. Nevertheless, only a fraction of the peasantry was covered by this agrarian reform.

While pressures from peasant organizations exerted some influence on the middle-class leadership of the state, its agrarian policies and its attitude toward peasant organizations were primarily determined by the need to gain popular support against external and internal opponents. During the years between 1923 and 1928—when the Mexican leadership faced extremely strong opposition from the United States, rebellious army troops, and the Church—land reform reached its largest degree of development prior to 1934.

Between 1929 and 1933—when conflicts between the Mexican and the American governments, United States business interests, as well as the Mexican Church and military subsided—agrarian reform became more and more limited.

The years between 1934 and 1940, when under the presidency of Lazaro Cardenas land redistribution reached an all-time peak, were also years when the Mexican government posed the greatest challenge to the United States and Great Britain by nationalizing the holdings of many foreign business interests, above all, the oil companies.

To what degree the need to gain popular support for a possible international and national crisis and to what degree pressure from peasant organizations influenced the government's policy is a matter for further research. It seems clear, nevertheless, that, with the exception of the Zapatista movement in central Mexico between 1910 and 1920, nonpeasants controlled and decisively influenced the peasant movements as well as the pace and direction of agrarian reform.

1. The agrarian aspects of the Mexican Revolution are described in: Frank Tannenbaum; *The Mexican Agrarian Revolution* (New York, 1929); Nathan L. Whetten; *Rural Mexico,* (Chicago, 1948); Centro de Investigaciones Agrarias; *Estructura Agraria y Desarrollo Agrícola de Mexico,* 3 vols. (Mexico, 1970).

2. James W. Willkie, *The Mexican Revolution: Federal Expenditure and Social Change since 1910* (Berkeley and Los Angeles, 1967), p. 188 ff.

3. Tannenbaum; *Mexican Agrarian Revolution,* chap. 1. For the history and role of the free Indian villages in the colonial period see; Charles Gibson, *The Aztecs under Spanish Rule* (Stanford, 1964).

4. Friedrich Katz, "Labor conditions in Porfirian Mexico: Some trends and tendencies;" *Hispanic American Historical Review,* Feb. 1974, vol. 54, no. 1

5. Paul Friedrich; *Agrarian Revolt in a Mexican Village,* (Englewood Cliffs, New Jersey, 1970).

6. See Robert Ricard; *The Spiritual Conquest of Mexico* (Berkeley and Los Angeles: University of California Press, 1967).

7. This passivity should not be overrated. While missionary penetration of Indian regions was frequently peaceful, most mission Indians staged uprisings at one time or another against the religious orders. The Tarahumara Indians rose four times—in 1632, 1648, 1690, and 1697. The Yaquis revolted in 1740 against the Jesuits. The causes for these revolts were not identical. The Tarahumaras rose against the Jesuits because the latter tried to remove them from their mountain homes and to concentrate them in large villages, called *reducciones.* The Yaquis did not object to these *reducciones,* which they maintained long after the missionaries left, but to increased Jesuit exactions destined to finance new missions in California. For a description of these uprisings see Joseph Neumann, *Revolte des Indiens Tarahumaras* (Paris, 1969). Data about the Yaqui uprising of 1740 was supplied by Evelyn Hu-DeHart, who is completing a dissertation on the history of the Yaqui nation.

8. See Katz, "Labor Conditions in Porfirian Mexico."

9. Departamento Agrario; Mexico, "Dirección de Terrenos Nacionales," Expediente 161.

10. For the links between the building of railroads and expropriation of communal lands see, John H. Coatsworth; "Railroads and the Concentration of Landownership in the Early Porfiriato;" *Hispanic American Historical Review,* Feb. 1974.

11. Evelyn Hu-DeHart; "Pacification of the Yaquis in the Late Porfiriato: Development and Implications;" *Hispanic American Historical Review,* Feb. 1974.

12. Moisés Gonzalez Navarro; *Raza y Tierra; La Guerra de Castas y el Henequén* (Mexico, 1970), p. 87.

13. John Womack; *Zapata and the Mexican Revolution* (New York, 1970); Francois Chevalier; "Un Factor Decisivo de la Revolución Agraria de Mexico; El Levantamiento de Zapata (1911–1919)," *Cuadernos Americanos,* Vol. 113, Nov. 6, 1960; Gildardo Magaña and Carlos Pérez Guerrero; *Emiliano Zapata y el Agrarismos en Mexico,* 5 vols. (Mexico, 1951–52).

14. Hu-DeHart; "Pacification of the Yaquis."

15. *Memorias de Don Adolfo de la Huerta según su propio dictado* (Mexico, 1957) pp. 11–20.

16. Departamento Agrario, Mexico, Dirección de Terrenos Nacionales Diversos, Expediente 2. Letter of the Inhabitants of Namiquipa to President Díaz, July 25, 1908.

17. Departamento Agrario, Mexico, Dirección de Terrenos Nacionales Diversos, Expediente 37 × 5. Junta Directiva de los Vecinos de Cuchillo Parado to the Secretario de Fomento, Jan. 10, 1903.

18. Chihuahua became a kind of estate of the Terrazas family. Terrazas became governor of Chihuahua in May 1903. In August 1904 he turned the governorship over to his son-in-law, Enrique Creel. Creel was succeeded in 1910 by Terrazas' son, Alberto. See Francisco Almada; *Diccionario de Historia, Geografía y Biografía Chihuahuenses* (Chihuahua, 1960).

19. Departamento Agrario; Dirección de Terrenos Nacionales Diversos, Exp. 178. Letter of the Inhabitants of Namiquipa to President Díaz, July 20, 1908.

20. Departamento Agrario; Dirección de Terrenos Nacionales Diversos, Expediente 75–1407. Letter of Porfirio Talamantes, representing the Inhabitants of Janos to President Díaz, Aug. 22, 1908.

21. Francisco de P. Ontiveros; *Toribio Ortega y la Brigada Gonzalez Ortega* (Chihuahua, 1914).

22. Armando B. Chavez *Diccionario de Hombres de la Revolución en Chihuahua* (Chihuahua, 1973).

23. Alberto Calzadíaz Barrera, *Hechos relaes de la Revolución,* vol. 3 (Mexico, 1972).

24. *Anuario estadístico del Estado de Chihuahua 1904–1910* (Chihuahua, 1911).

25. Katz; "Labor Conditions in Porfirian Mexico."

26. Harold D. Sims; *Espejo de Caciques: Los Terrazas de Chihuahua* (Historia Mexicana No. 71, 1969).

27. Francisco Almada; *Vida, Proceso, Muerte de Abraham Gonzalez* (Mexico, 1967); William H. Beezley; *Insurgent Governor Abraham Gonzalez and the Mexican Revolution in Chihuahua* (Lincoln, Nebraska, 1973).

28. Michael C. Meyer; *Mexican Rebel: Pascual Orozco and the Mexican Revolution* (Lincoln, Nebraska, 1967).

29. Martin Luis Guzmán; *Memorias de Pancho Villa* (Mexico, 1968); Federico Cervantes, *Francisco Villa y la Revolución* (Mexico, 1960).

30. The similarities of some agrarian aspects of the French, Russian, and Chinese revolutions should not obscure the great differences between them. The main beneficiaries of the dissolution of the French estates during the Revolution were wealthy peasants and urban bourgeois. In Russia and China the revolutionaries made great efforts to grant land to the poor peasants. See Barrington Moore, Jr., *Social Origins of Dictatorship and Democracy Lord and Peasant in the Making of the Modern World* (Boston, 1966).

31. See Robert Freeman Smith; *The United States and Revolutionary Nationalism in Mexico 1916–1932* (Chicago, 1972).

32. Friedrich Katz; *Deutschland, Diaz und die Mexikanische Revolution* (Berlin, 1964), p. 237 ff.

33. R. F. Smith; *United States and Revolutionary Nationalism,* p. 145.

34. J. M. Maytorena; *Algunas Verdades acerca del General Obregón* (Los Angeles, 1919).

35. Francisco R. Almada; *La Revolución en el Estado de Chihuahua* (Mexico, 1971), p. 89.

36. Armando de María y Campos; *La Vida del General Lucio Blanco* (Mexico 1963), p. 53 ff.

37. Friedrich Katz; "Agrarian changes in Northern Mexico in the Period of Villista rule 1913–1915," paper delivered at the 4th International Congress of Mexican Studies (Santa Monica, California, 1973).

38. Hans Werner Tobler; *Alvaro Obregón und die Anfaenge der Mexikanischen Agrarreform, Agrarpolitik und Agrarkonflikt, 1921–1924; Jahrbuch fuer Geschichte von Staat, Wirtschaft und Gesellschaft Lateinamerikas;* vol. 8 (Koeln-Wien, 1971).

39. Womack; *Zapata and the Mexican Revolution,* p. 224 ff.

40. There obviously was one group of the peasantry, the inhabitants of former military colonies, part of whose lands had been taken from them who had clear agrarian aims. Nevertheless, there is no evidence of land seizure by these groups or of pressure on the state government for an immediate return of their former holdings. One reason for their attitude may have been the fact that a large number of their inhabitants were involved in the revolutionary army and were fighting far away from their native villages. For these men, who not only hoped to regain the lands their communities had lost but also expected to be granted lands to reward them for their participation in the Revolution, an agrarian reform should only have taken place upon their return from the war.

41. Womack; *Zapata and the Mexican Revolution.* For Villa's position see Francisco Almada; *La Revolución en el Estado de Chihuahua,* vol. 4, (Mexico, 1964), p. 212.

42. Carranza stated this very clearly in his address to the Mexican Congress on April 15, 1917. Venustiano Carranza, Informe del C. Venustiano Carranza, Primer Jefe del Ejército Constitucionalista, Encargado del Poder Ejécutivo de la República. Leído ante el Congreso de la Unión en la sesión del 15 de Abril de 1917 (Mexico, 1917).

43. Nelson Reed; *The Caste War of Yucatán* (Stanford, 1964), p. 260 f.; Salvador Alvarado; *Mi actuación revolucionaria en el Estado de Yucatán* (Mexico, 1919).

44. Heather Fowler Salamini; "The Agrarian Revolution in the State of Veracruz, 1920–1940: The Role of Peasant Organizations," Ph.D. dissertation, The American University, 1970.

45. This policy is described by Anatoli Shulgovski; *Mexico en la Encrucijada de su Historia* (Mexico, 1966).

African Peasantries and Revolutionary Change

JOHN S. SAUL

IN THE PAST MANY SOCIAL SCIENTISTS HAVE BEEN RELUCTANT TO use the term "peasant" with reference to African cultivators. More recently a body of literature has emerged that, in seeking to theorize the most important trends in rural Africa, has found the notion of the peasantry to be a particularly illuminating one. Some brief reference to this latter emphasis, and to the rationale that sustains it, will need to be made here. But the main thrust of this paper lies elsewhere —in a discussion of the conditions (socioeconomic, ideological, organizational) under which the African peasantry, so identified, becomes a force for radical transformation of the status quo of colonialism and neocolonialism in contemporary Africa. It is worth emphasizing at the outset that the latter is no mere academic concern. In the two concrete situations that we shall explore—the Portuguese colony of Mozambique and the independent country of Tanzania—it is the conscious attempt to engage the peasants in precisely such revolutionary activity that has been one of the most striking features of recent political and socioeconomic developments there. In Mozambique the success of this strategy has been crowned by the presentation of a particularly dramatic challenge to Portuguese colonial hegemony. In Tanzania the ultimate effectiveness of that country's challenge to neocolonalism is more open to doubt, but the intense interest of the effort to construct a new, socialist Tanzania on a popular base of active and self-conscious "workers and peasants" cannot be denied.

Peasants and Revolution

Revolutionary theory has evinced much skepticism concerning the peasantry—a skepticism rooted in the classics of Marxism and, most dramatically, in Marx's own oft-quoted description of the peasants as being merely like a "sack of potatoes," divided and demobilized.[1] Yet peasants in the twentieth century have become a revolutionary force in ways that Marx, necessarily, could not predict. There are those who cling steadfastly to the classical view, of course, arguing that the proletariat, by virtue of its participation in the centralizing and collectivizing logic of modern industry, remains the sole and indispensable guarantor of genuine revolution. Those who, like Nigel Harris, press the point most fiercely, are aided in so doing by a definition of socialism (the end-product of any such genuine revolution) that excludes every existing country from that category.[2] Others, less concerned to ignore the claims of, say, a country like China to revolutionary achievement are, concomitantly, more charitable toward the peasantry. Indeed, Malcolm Caldwell, vigorously criticizing Harris's position and making, among other points, "the simple factual assertion that the peasantry played the decisive role in the Chinese revolution," has gone so far as to conclude:

> we may be sure that the peoples of Africa, Asia, and Latin America themselves alone can transform their own lives. Since the vast majority of these people are peasants, the future must lie in their hands, whether it accords with one's preconceived theories or not. . . . In the world of today, the poor, the dissatisfied and the unprivileged are peasants: therefore "the peasants alone are revolutionary for they have nothing to lose and everything to gain!"[3]

It is not necessary here to exhaust the general debate being rehearsed (and, it would seem, unduly polarized) in the exchange between Harris and Caldwell. As a first approximation, it is sufficient to remind ourselves of Trotsky's dictum: "Without a guiding organization the energy of the masses would dissipate like steam not enclosed in a piston box. But nonetheless what moves things is not the piston, or the box, but the steam."[4] For one cannot examine the course of recent history without affirming that peasants have provided much of the steam for revolutionary challenge to the status quo in this century. Why should this be so? Many Marxists emphasize that the expansion of the international capitalist system into less-developed areas of the world has been such as to displace certain crucial contradictions of that system from its center to its periphery.[5] And even a growing number of non-Marxist thinkers seek for answers to such a question in an understanding of imperialism. Thus, Eric Wolf, summarizing the lessons drawn from a careful survey of "peasant wars of the twentieth century," concludes that the historical experience that situates such wars "constitutes, in turn, the precipitate in the present of a great overriding cultural phenomenon, the worldwide spread and diffusion of a particular cultural system, that of North Atlantic capitalism."[6] Moreover, we shall see that it is precisely a concern with the historical emergence and further evolution of capitalist imperialism that is crucial to an identification of the peasantry (and other relevant actors) in an African setting.

Nonetheless, many misgivings expressed by Marx and others about the peasantry's likely contribution to revolution also have some validity. Parochialism cuts deep in the rural areas; the outlines of the broader exploitative environment, worldwide and territorial, that oppresses the peasant, are not easily perceived by him and as a result "the aggregate of small producers" constitute themselves only with difficulty as a group capable of "a shared consciousness and joint political action as a class."[7] Even if peasant political action (rather than apathetic resignation or preoccupation with quasi-traditional involvements closer to home) is forthcoming it may still prove either to be quite localized and isolated in its spontaneous expression, or else be forced too easily into channels of mere regional and ethnic self-assertiveness by a territorial leadership that divides in order that it may continue to rule. Moreover, most twentieth century revolutionaries aim at some kind of socialist transformation of the existing system, this being, ultimately, the only effective response to imperialism. The peasants' temptation to seek a resolution of the contradictions that confront him either by shoring up "traditional" aspects of the peasant economy or by attempting "petty-bourgeois" solutions that would further service his isolation—a redistribution of land designed to guarantee his own individual tenure and possible economic aggrandizement on that basis, for example—may make him a risky ally for such an enterprise.

This seems all the more likely to be the case when one considers the findings of Wolf and of Hamza Alavi—that it is the "middle peasant" rather than the poorest of peasants who is "initially the most militant element of the peasantry."[8] Yet counterrevolutionary results are not inevitable. Alavi does observe that "when the movement in the countryside advances to a revolutionary stage they (the middle peasants) may move away from the revolutionary movement" since "their social perspective is limited by their class position." Nonetheless, he suggests that this is only true "unless their fears are allayed and they are drawn into the process of cooperative endeavour"! Moreover, poorer peasants, who have an even greater stake in structural transformation, gradually can become mobilized for action as well—and carry the revolutionary process further.[9] Indeed, what is demonstrated by the introduction of various qualifications to the more roseate picture of the peasantry painted by Caldwell is merely the need to avoid falling back on romantic illusions about the inevitable and unequivocal *spontaneity* of peasant involvement in revolution. It becomes clear that if peasant action is to service such a revolution—to manifest full confidence and a sense of efficacy, to acquire effectively national focus, and to set in train a comprehensive transformation of society—*political work* must come to mediate it and help to define its thrust.

We return by this route to Trotsky's metaphor: a "piston box" is also necessary in order to harness the steam of peasant discontent. Again, one of Wolf's formulations is suggestive: "Peasants often harbour a deep sense of injustice, but this sense of injustice must be given shape and expression in organization before it can become active on the political scene; and it is obvious that not every callow agitator will find welcome hearing in village circles, traditionally suspicious of outsiders." Like Wolf, we must be "greatly aware of the importance of groups which mediate between the peasants and the larger society of which he forms a part." However, this emphasis too would be misleading if the capacity of the peasants to play an active role in the process of politicizing their grievances were to be understated. In fact, the vital *contradiction* between organization/leadership on the one hand and participation/spontaneity on the other is not one that can be evaded or suppressed—both aspects are essential. If effective methods of political work are used, it is merely a contradiction that can be *resolved,* over time, in a manner that contributes to further revolutionary advance.

In recent times, "people's war" has been the technique that has

89

most satisfactorily realized this goal, this effective blending of both leadership from above and spontaneity from below. Selden has stated this point clearly with reference to Vietnam and China, and his formulation is worth quoting at length:[10]

Out of the ashes of military strife which enveloped China and Vietnam in protracted wars of liberation emerged a radically new vision of man and society and a concrete approach to development. Built on foundations of participation and community action which challenge elite domination, this approach offers hope of more *humane* forms of development and of effectively overcoming the formidable barriers to the transformation of peasant societies. In the base areas and consolidated war zones in which the movement enjoyed its fullest growth, the redefinition of community began in the resistance to a foreign invader and continued in the struggle to overcome domestic problems of poverty and oppression. People's war implies more than a popular guerrilla struggle for national independence; it impinges directly on the full scope of rural life. In the course of a people's war, local communities defined in response to the imperatives of defense and social change may be effectively integrated in national movements. The very intensity of the wartime experience contributes to rapid development of consciousness and organization. In people's war peasants cease to be the passive pawns of landlords and officials or to fatalistically accept the verdict of a harsh natural environment. Where the primary resource of insurgent movements in man [*sic*], and where active commitment is the *sine qua non* of success, the sharing of common hardships and hopes creates powerful bonds among resisters and between leaders and led. In the new institutions which emerge locally in the course of the resistance, to an unprecedented degree peasants begin to secure active control of their economic and political destinies.

We shall see that this is precisely the pattern that has emerged in Mozambique in the course of the liberation struggle against Portuguese colonialism. In Tanzania the situation is more complicated. There the leadership, or one section of it, has also made some effort to forge "new bonds of unity in which the very definitions of leader and led are recast and the beginnings of a new social base are created." But it is doing so "in cold blood," as it were—from within the framework of established structures, rather than in the heat of a convulsive upheaval. It is obvious that the making of a peasant-based "revolution" under such circumstances presents anomalies—and, as we shall see, it is indeed proving to be a difficult task.

African Peasantries

Who are "the peasants" in Tanzania and Mozambique, then? Indeed, "are African cultivators to be called peasants?," as a well-known article on rural Africa once asked.[11] It is worth noting that this has been a subject of some controversy in the literature, though it is a controversy that easily degenerates into a mere word game. In the first instance, the debate has seemed most concerned with the nature of "traditional" Africa; moreover, the latter has all too often been ossified and discussed by social scientists as some kind of "anthropological present" in a manner that can foreclose discussion of the *real present* of colonialism and neocolonialism. Even with reference to precontact Africa there may have been more peasantlike dimensions of the rural situation than has sometimes been assumed.[12] But the more immediately relevant argument of a number of recent writers is that, whatever the case for an earlier Africa, the incursion of imperialism and particularly of formal colonialism has gradually forced a large proportion of rural dwellers in Africa to take on the characteristics of a peasantry. As Woods and I have argued elsewhere,[13] this way of construing the majority of rural Africans is important. First, it fits neatly within the kind of broad analytical framework that seems best suited to identifying and explaining the overall patterns of change and development in contemporary Africa. Second, the concept quite accurately pinpoints characteristics of rural Africans that bear a family resemblance to peasant characteristics as identified elsewhere; it thus enables students of Africa, and political activists there, to collect data and theorize experience alongside others concerned about the problematic of the peasantry in other parts of the world. These two points can be briefly documented.

The key historical factor in defining the shape of contemporary Africa has been its forced insertion, as a dependency, within the broader Europe-centered imperial system.[14] And "despite the existence of some pre-figurings of a peasant class in earlier periods, it is more fruitful to view the creation of an African peasantry . . . as being primarily the result of the interaction between an international capitalist economic system and traditional socioeconomic systems, within the context of territorially defined colonial political systems." Ken Post has described the process of "peasantization" in West Africa in similar terms, citing Trotsky's "Law of Uneven and Combined Development" and emphasizing the economic, political, and cultural dimensions of the process that subordinates "communal cultivators and such precolonial peasants as there were" to that broader system:

> Whatever their differences, it is true to say that all the colonial powers in Western Africa greatly extended the market principle, to the point where the impersonal forces of the world market dominated the lives of millions, and imposed a State where none had been before or to supersede indigenous ones. The African quest for western education and the issue of assimilation amply demonstrate the presence of a new "great" culture. It would appear, then, that many of the conditions for the existence of a peasantry were suddenly created, but from outside and quite independently of the processes of internal differentiation in origin, though the internal factors had important influences upon the final form of these conditions.[15]

In validating this perspective, Post is particularly concerned to demonstrate that "surplus" is extracted from the African rural population within such a structure—by the "levying of taxes and other dues by the state," for example, and by unequal terms of exchange for agricultural produce. Finally, Derman has made closely related points—with reference in particular to the role of the state in peasantizing cultivators—when he criticizes the views of those anthropologists who continue to withold the term "peasantry" from such rural dwellers and instead see them as "subsistence oriented cultivators in the process of becoming farmers"! In Derman's view, this ignores the fact that "the state—both colonial and post-colonial—remains highly exploitative of the rural peasants or cultivators. African peasants are coming to form an increasingly subordinate segment of the population, a trend which began during the colonial era."[16] This too is a suggestive perception, and is entirely accurate.

Balancing the fact of such structural subordination within the wider political and economic systems of Africa, is a second feature, one which is equally necessary in order to confirm the peasant character of such cultivators (particularly in comparative terms): "the importance to the peasantry of the family economy."

> Thus peasants are those whose ultimate security and subsistence lies in their having certain rights in land and in the labor of family members on the land, but who are involved, through rights and obligations, in a wider economic system which includes the participation of nonpeasants. The fact that for peasants ultimate security and subsistence rests upon maintaining rights in land and rights in family labor is an important determinant shaping and restricting their social action. It is also the characteristic which peasants share with "primitive agriculturists," though not with capitalist farmers. For while the capitalist farmer may *appear* to depend upon his land, he is not *forced* to rely upon these in the last instance; he has alternative potential sources of security and investment. What the peasant does share, in general terms, with the capitalist farmer (though not with the primitive agriculturalist) is his integration into a complex social structure characterized by stratification and economic differentiation.

In Africa it is also possible to keep the term "peasant" flexible enough to include pastoralists within it, since they "are subject to the same kind of political and economic forces as their predominantly agricultural brethren and since their productive economy (inasmuch as it involves rights to, and control over, family herds) is based on a similar kind of 'homestead' principle." And, more controversially, to include migrant laborers. The latter inclusion is justified by the stake which such migrants retain in, precisely, "the family economy." While some peasants will seek to guarantee the surplus demanded by the broader social structure by means of attaching a cash-crop component to their basically subsistence-oriented cultivation, others will seek to do so by periods of time spent laboring in mines, plantations, and urban centers. But they do so without relinquishing their family's claim to an agricultural stake in the rural community. The logic of the migrant's position within the overall system remains the same as that of the cash-cropper—at least in the short run, while both remain peasants.

Note the latter phrase. It is important, for the logic of continued capitalist penetration should be, of course, to phase out the African peasantry even as it creates it. At the one end of the spectrum peasants who start to generate surpluses in the sphere of cash-cropping may become, in time, *capitalist farmers*. And migrants (as well as those who start to sell their labor power locally to supplement their subsistence agricultural activities) may become, in time, more definitely *proletarianized*. In short, these two tendencies "can chip away at the peasantry, pulling it in different directions." At the same time, the pace at which this apparent "logic" now works itself out must not be overestimated. The realities of Africa's continuing dependence means that peripheral capitalism in Africa tends to produce merely further underdevelopment rather than a total capitalist transformation of countries there. As a result, and as Colin Leys has written in demonstrating the *increased* rate of peasantization in Kenya (itself one of the most seemingly dynamic of dependencies in Africa):

> Analytically speaking, the peasantry in Africa may be best seen as a transitional class, in between the period of primitive cultivators living in independent communities and that of capitalist development in which peasants are restratified into capitalists and proletarians; but under the conditions of growth of neocolonialism, it seems clear that in Kenya at least the stage during which the peasantry itself goes through a process of development, and develops its own pattern of relationships with the elite, may be fairly prolonged.[17]

It could be argued, therefore, that the African peasantry is not composed of peasants quite like those in earlier, historically more progressive, capitalist systems (as analyzed by Barrington Moore) "over whom the wave of progress is about to roll."[18] Perhaps this will give them more of an opportunity to shape their own futures.[19]

Two main points follow from the analysis thus far presented.

94

There is *a peasantry* in Africa—large numbers of rural Africans caught, by international capitalism and colonial and postcolonial state structures, between subsistence cultivation and the fates that capitalism might eventually hold in store for them. In this reality of common "peasant-hood," there is the potential grounds for "shared consciousness and shared political action" against the broader structures that have come to dominate and exploit them. The multinational corporations and the national elites, along with their representatives in the rural areas themselves, would be the legitimate targets of action to redress such a situation. It is in this reality that there lies the promise of a peasant revolution and possibly the seeds of socialism—a promise to the analysis of which we will return in the next section.

But what we have said so far also suggests that there are *peasantries* in Africa—these representing the wide range of variation in the way the peasantized have become involved in the broader imperial systems. Or in the terms used by Lionel Cliffe, they represent the varying "articulations of modes of production," different ways in which "historically and geographically specific and various modes" of production in Africa have "articulated," or interacted, with "the increasingly dominant capitalist mode." This variation, in turn, means that

> in each territory we can distinguish a number of peasantries who are differentiated according to locality—some localities being labor exporting, some food-crop exporting, some cash-crop exporting and some with varying proportions of each. . . . [In addition], the dynamic of capitalist development tends to introduce a further element which cuts across the differentiation of peasants by locality with a differentiation based on the degree of involvement in the cash economy. This involves . . . the possible movements toward proletarianization of migrant labor on the one hand and toward capitalist agriculture on the other.

Since, unlike certain other parts of the globe, African territories lacked some broadly comparable precapitalist structure (e.g., feudalism) spread over a large area, but instead comprised an extraordinary range of precapitalist social formations, it seems probable that the range of "articulation of modes of production" that springs from capitalist incursion is, if anything, more varied in Africa than elsewhere. To elicit even a roughly common response and common level of consciousness from "peasants" so diversified is concomitantly difficult.

Revolution in Africa

What of revolution, then? In the first section, we quoted Malcolm Caldwell's general conclusion to his argument concerning "the revolutionary role of the peasantry": "In the world of today, the poor, the dissatisfied and the unprivileged are peasants. Therefore 'the peasants alone are revolutionary, for they have nothing to lose and everything to gain.' " Significantly, the quotation which Caldwell uses here is from Fanon—and Fanon was writing about Africa.[20] But Fanon's enthusiasm is not fully shared by others—the late Amilcar Cabral, one of Africa's outstanding revolutionaries, for example. "Obviously", he says, "the group with the greatest interest in the struggle is the peasantry, given the nature of the various different societies in Guinea . . . and the various degrees of exploitation to which they are subjected." However, things cannot merely be left to rest there, for "the question is not simply one of objective interest." Cabral then proceeds

> to broach one key problem, which is of enormous importance for us, as we are a country of peasants, and that is the problem of whether or not the peasantry represents the main revolutionary force. A distinction must be drawn between a physical force and a revolutionary force; physically, the peasantry is a great force in Guinea; it is almost the whole of the population, it controls the nation's wealth, it is the peasantry which produces; but we know from experience what trouble we had convincing the peasantry to fight.[21]

Leys, the academic observer, states a related point even more forcefully in concluding his analysis of Kenya and of revolutionary prospects there. For "as writers such as Moore, Alavi and Wolf have shown, it generally requires a rare combination of tyranny and misery to produce a peasant revolt, let alone a peasant revolution; short of which the clientelist political structures characteristic of peasant society have a resilience which can easily be underestimated."

Many of the grounds for skepticism about the revolutionary vocation of the peasantry that were asserted in general terms in the first section apply to Africa—in some instances with even greater force. In many parts of the world rural dwellers are, in effect, peasantized twice over, first by the workings of some form of feudal system and second by the further structural subordination that arises from the insertion of that feudal system within a colonial-cum-international capitalist framework. However, exploitation and subordination are rendered more intangible in many, though of course not all, African settings because of the absence of landlords and quasi-feudal relationships at the point of direct production. This can have the result of depersonalizing and distancing the overall exploitative system, thus diffusing discontent.[22] Also population pressure on the land has not been as great in rural Africa, relatively speaking, as on other continents, and the visible threat to peasant status (especially to prospects for guaranteeing subsistence) from that quarter not quite so pressing.

Additionally, while it is true that few but the most isolated of Africans remain untouched by the peasantization process, the unfulfilled nature of this process, its unevenness and its relative recentness have left standing, perhaps more firmly than elsewhere, important vestiges of precapitalist social networks and cultural preoccupations—particularly a range of variations on the kinship relationship and upon the theme of ethnic identification—which mesh closely with the survival of the subsistence agricultural core of the system. At the same time some of those who do begin to break more definitely with the attributes of peasanthood do so under the influence of burgeoning petty-capitalist aspirations, rather than by notions of the collective improvement of the rural dwellers' lot. In making links with the world beyond the village such elements may find their most natural allies among the new elites who control state power.

But this—the aligning of itself with energetic capitalists-in-the-making in the villages—is only one way in which the neocolonial state defuses the possibility of peasant class consciousness. Equally important, the "quasi-traditional" attributes of peasanthood can also be warped in such a way as to service the functioning of Africa's neocolonial systems by those who benefit from them. The key, as Leys has argued, lies in the politics of patron-client relationships, broadly defined. In the first instance, peasants can be tied into the system by links with others above them in the heirarchy (these often being more privileged kinsmen) and by such small benefits as trickle down to them in this manner. In addition, politicians operating in the national arena have often come to play what is, in effect, a similar role over a broader terrain—that of super-patrons with their tribes as their clients. For "tribalism" (the politicization of ethnicity which is all too characteristic a pathology of dependent Africa) does not spring primarily from the bare fact of the existence of cultural differences between peoples. Rather, it has been teased into life, first by the divide-and-rule tactics of colonialism and by the uneven development in the economic sphere that colonialism also facilitates and, second, by the ruling petty-bourgeoisie of the postcolonial period. The latter, too, seek to divide and rule—better from their point of view that peasants should conceive the national pie as being divided, competitively, between regions and tribes, rather than (as is in fact much more clearly the case) between classes. Moreover, as individuals, they are moved to mobilize tribal constituencies behind themselves, using this as a bargaining counter in the struggle for power against other members of the ruling circles.[23]

Can African peasants come to be something more than mere pawns in the unattractive game of underdevelopment? Certainly peasants have not always been passive elements in recent African history. Their discontent often flared into overt action, revealing in the process ironies that Fanon has pinpointed (and Kilson and others have documented):

What is the reaction of the nationalist parties of this eruption of peasant masses into the nationalist struggle? . . . As a whole they treat this new element as a sort of manna from heaven, and pray to goodness that it'll go on falling. They make the most of the manna, but do not attempt to organize the rebellion. They don't send leaders into the countryside to educate the people politically, or to increase their awareness or put the struggle on to a higher level. All they do is to hope that, carried onwards by its own momentum, the action of the people will not come to a standstill. There is no contamination of the rural movement by the urban movement; each develops according to its own dialectic.[24]

Of course, the very diversity of peasantries also makes the "putting of the struggle on a higher level" a crucial necessity. For different peasantries have felt, immediately, different kinds of grievances against the colonial system. The nationalist movements described by Fanon tended merely to accumulate the support of such aggrieved peasantries around the lowest common denominator of a demand for political independence, rather than generalizing their grievances into a critique of imperial and capitalist reality more adequately defined. The leadership elements, so soon to inherit the established structures, had little interest in encouraging the development of a broader vision, of allaying fears and drawing peasants "into the process of cooperative endeavor" (as Alavi suggested to be one possible denouement of peasant upsurge effectively politicized).

Instead, the mere Africanization of peripheral capitalism proceeded apace. Yet, as Nyerere has argued, this has had little ultimately to offer the vast mass of the peasantry:

sooner of later, the people will lose their enthusiasm and will look upon the independent government as simply another new ruler which they should avoid as much as possible. Provided it has been possible to avoid any fundamental upset in their traditional economic and social conditions, they will then sink back into apathy—until the next time someone is able to convince them that their own efforts can lead to an improvement in their lives![25]

Moreover, this latter possibility suggested by Nyerere has occasionally become a reality. The Congo of the mid-sixties provides an example—glimpsed in Pierre Mulele's activities in the Kwilu and in the People's Republic of the Eastern Congo. Of the latter Gerard-Libois has written:

99

the insurrections which led to the creation of the People's Republic were first of all a revolt of impoverished and exploited peasants for whom the enemy was not only the foreign colonialist but above all those Congolese who had monopolized all the fruits of independence, and also those policemen, administrators and even teachers who served the new class and sought to imitate its style of life. . . . [T]he rebellion was . . . , for all its limitations, the hope of a new independence, fundamentally different from the first, and through which the wealth of the Congo would accrue to the poorest and in which a new, genuinely decolonized African society would come into being.[26]

Such activities easily lost focus, and the character of the Mobutist denouement in the Congo (now Zaire) is well known. Whether more recent attempts to revive a revolutionary challenge in that country (seen in the work of the Congolese Marxist Revolutionary Party, for example) will be any more successful remains to be seen, but something of the nature of the "stream" which does exist at the base of contemporary African societies could be discerned in Kwilu. In addition, broad trends like the growth of population pressure may come, over time, to further exacerbate such tensions in rural Africa.[27]

At base, then, the contradiction between the peasantry and established structures, worldwide and continental/territorial, remains. We quoted Cabral at the outset of this section. It is worth continuing that quotation, drawn from his analysis of the Guinean peasantry: "All the same, in certain parts of the country and among certain groups we found a warm welcome, even right from the start. In other groups and in other areas all this had to be won." Nonetheless, it has been won: in Guinea-Bissau the peasants have become an active agency for a deep-cutting revolution. Of course, the overall structure within which the achievement of Cabral and his PAIGC has been realized is a particularly anomalous one. Portuguese "ultra-colonialism," even more cruel and unyielding than other colonialisms in Africa, provided precisely that "rare combination of tyranny and misery" that Leys mentioned as being an important prerequisite of a peasant revolt. Moreover, it is obvious that anticolonial nationalism could be used as an initial ideological rallying cry for revolution in Guinea much more unequivocally than in a postcolonial situation;

in Nyerere's words, it is "another thing when you have to remove your own people from the position of exploiters."[28] Yet Cabral emphasizes again and again that, despite even these "advantages" in Guinea, hard *political work* has still been necessary in order to realize a peasant base for struggle. How much more this is likely to be the case elsewhere in Africa!

Cabral describes the nature of such political work carefully and suggestively in his writings. Particularly important have been the cadres who came to play the role of catalyst of the Guinean revolution. They were drawn initially from the petty-bourgeois stratum and from semiproletarianized urban hangers-on, beginning their work as what Gorz has termed an "external vanguard" vis-à-vis the peasants. But they have become, with time and with the effective resolution of the contradiction between leadership and participation, much more of an "internal vanguard"[29] a development that has also meant the sharing of authority with new leadership elements thrown up by the the newly mobilized peasants themselves as the peasants' own confidence and commitment to the struggle has grown. Obviously, a number of further questions arise from this: How are the *different* peasantries likely to be geared into such struggle (note that some provided a "warm welcome" to Cabral and his colleagues, others not)? What kind of "piston box" of organization and ideology, constructed by the revolutionaries themselves, can most effectively facilitate this process? By turning to an examination of the situation in Mozambique, similar in certain important respects to that in Guinea, we can begin, though only begin, to answer these questions.

Mozambique

The two questions just mentioned are not separate, however. The Mozambican case demonstrates the importance of examining both the nature of the peasantry as a potential base for revolution and the nature of the presumed revolutionary organization—in the case, the Mozambique Liberation Front (FRELIMO)—in considering recent developments there. But it is probably even more essential to examine the dialectical relationship established between the two—between peasantry and political organization—for it is this relationship that has defined the forward momentum of the Mozambique revolution.

That the peasants are an essential base there can be no doubt. Eduardo Mondlane, the first president of FRELIMO who was assassinated by the Portuguese in 1969, made this point clearly:

> Both the agitation of the intellectuals and the strikes of the urban labor force were doomed to failure, because in both cases it was the action only of a tiny isolated group. For a government like Portugal's, which has set its face against democracy and is prepared to use extremes of brutality to crush opposition, it is easy to deal with such isolated pockets of resistance. It was the very failure of these attempts, however, and the fierce repression which followed, that made this clear and prepared the ground for more widely based action. The urban population of Mozambique amounts altogether to less than half a million. A nationalist movement without firm roots in the countryside could never hope to succeed.[30]

More recently, Marcellino dos Santos, FRELIMO's vice-president, has described that countryside along lines that are essentially similar to those elaborated upon in this paper. Beginning with a juxtaposition of "two societies" in Mozambique, that which "contains capitalist relationships" and that of "the traditional type—a sort of subsistence economy," he proceeds to dissolve this distinction in his subsequent discussion:

> But these two societies do not exist in isolation from one another; they are entirely linked. Why? Where do these people who work in the plantations come from? All those people who work within the capitalist sector come from the traditional sector. And most of them do not remain permanently outside the traditional sector because, for instance, many of them go to work on the plantations for a maximum of two years and they then come back to the village and to the traditional system. So that is the main link—going back and forth. Then there are those people who do not become absorbed into the capitalist system but who are nevertheless related to it. For instance, the people who produce for themselves must sell their produce in the market, mainly food like grain, cashew nuts. They are forced into the market system to find the cash for colonial-imposed taxes and to

purchase commodities which they do not produce themselves. So these two societies are linked and on many levels the persons comprising the two societies are the same.[31]

It will be readily apparent that Dos Santos is discussing what we have seen to be the African peasantry.

It has been an African peasantry pitchforked into existence and sustained in its "transitional" state by methods even more brutal than those employed by other colonialisms. Mondlane documents many of these methods in his book, discussing cash-cropping peasantries for whom the enforced cultivation of cotton and the rigging of government price schedules have introduced great hardship, and even more mercilessly exploited labor-supplying peasantries over the years by a complex system of virtual forced labor. It is precisely the systematic nature of such repressive practices that led Perry Anderson to speak of "Portuguese ultra-colonialism."[32] Small wonder that peasants periodically had given expression to their grievances even before the mounting of a comprehensive political challenge to colonialism. Thus, in Mondlane's words, "some developments in the countryside which took place in the period just preceding the formation of FRELIMO were of enormous importance." In the northern region around Mueda, for example, such activity centered upon efforts to organize a cooperative and obtain better terms for produce delivered to the colonial government; when peasants demonstrated peacefully in support of this program at Mueda in 1960, five hundred were shot down by the Portuguese.

Grievances there certainly have been and continue to be. Nor does it require any elaborate proof to demonstrate that they provide tinder for peasant action. Nonetheless, my own experience in the liberated areas of Mozambique in 1972 permits me to speak with some added confidence on the subject.[33] Traveling among the people of Tete Province with FRELIMO guerrillas, I had the opportunity to attend a number of political meetings and to hear the themes stressed both by FRELIMO militants and by ordinary peasants. A pinpointing of the economic linkages mentioned above—forced labor, a prejudicial system of cultivation—was joined with a precise enumeration of the abuses directly perpetrated by the Portuguese administration. Of the

103

latter, Portuguese taxation was a theme given particular prominence, its historically heavy role in the daily life of peasants being elucidated by FRELIMO cadres alongside an explanation of its importance in sustaining Portugal's ability to support economically its continued military presence. In effect, Mozambican peasants seemed themselves prepared to validate both Post's and Derman's earlier emphases—economic exploitation on the one hand, state power on the other—in defining their essentially subordinate position within previously established structures.

FRELIMO personnel also hinted at the existence of a range of variation in the response of different peasantries to revolutionary imperatives. In fact, it was obvious to me that this has been the subject of much serious analysis by the movement, since its strategy is precisely to establish deep political roots among the people of a given area by means of careful political work prior to launching armed activity. For this to be done, considerable knowledge of the stresses and strains in the local community under consideration is necessary. So much became particularly clear from discussions that I held with cadres who had long been active in such preparatory political work, as well as in the subsequent tasks of constructing FRELIMO-type social institutions in areas once they have been liberated. But, necessarily, concrete and detailed information on these matters was not forthcoming. It was suggested to me that the work of mobilization had gone much more easily in Tete than in Cabo Delgado and Niassa "because the people had had more experience of exploitation"—especially of the push of labor to other parts of Mozambique and to Rhodesia and South Africa.[34] This might seem to be evidence in support of Barnett's thesis that the "labor-exporting peasantry" has a "relatively high revolutionary potential" compared with the "cash-cropping peasantry" and the "marginal-subsistence peasantry."[35] But one cannot be categoric in these matters. Certainly the revolution has also advanced dramatically in Cabo and in Niassa where the latter types of peasantry are much more prominent, as well as in the cash-cropping areas of Tete itself. Similarly, in more immediately political terms, some chiefs seem to have reconciled themselves easily to the novel situation created by FRELIMO's presence, presenting few obstacles to the political involvement of "their people" on an entirely new basis, while others have defended themselves and Portuguese overrule with vigor. Historians will one day have important work to do in reconstructing more precisely such realities and the reasons for this range of variation.

Peasant "spontaneity" has been important then—and will probably become all the more so both as peasants respond negatively to such new and desperate last-ditch Portuguese strategies as the enforced strategic hamlet program and respond positively to the promise that life in the liberated areas increasingly exemplifies for them. Nonetheless, peasant spontaneity has not been a sufficient driving force for revolution in Mozambique. It has also taken an effective movement, FRELIMO, to bring the potential peasant base into meaningful and effective existence. I have discussed elsewhere that the evolution of FRELIMO itself has determined its character as a revolutionary movement. It was not inevitably such: "all those features characteristic of the brand of nationalism which has facilitated false decolonization elsewhere on the continent have been present in the Mozambican context."[36] There were elements in FRELIMO who were quite prone to aim primarily at their own elitist and entrepreneurial aggrandizement under the guise of nationalism and to refuse to integrate themselves with the peasant masses, preferring instead to demobilize the latter with ethnic and racial sloganeering.

However, "from the point of view of conservative members of the petty-bourgeois leadership of the Mozambican independence struggle there has been just one flaw in all this: in the context of a genuine liberation struggle this kind of nationalism, quite literally, *does not work* as it did for African leadership groups elsewhere on the continent." Portuguese intransigence meant that a stronger link with the people had to be forged in order to undertake effective guerrilla warfare. It was with this reality in mind that Sebastiao Mabote, FRELIMO's Chief of Operations (with whom I traveled in Mozambique), could say that the Portuguese had given Mozambique an opportunity other African states had missed—the opportunity to have a revolution. And that Eduardo Mondlane could say, shortly before his death and only half jokingly, that it would be almost a pity if the struggle were to succeed too quickly, "we are learning so much!"

Learning, for example, the necessity of enlisting the peasants more

105

actively in conscious support of the movement so that they would willingly undertake such *positive* tasks as maintaining the secrecy of FRELIMO activities in the face of colonialist pressure, as carriage of material and supply of produce, as direct enlistment in the army, reconnaissance and militia support work. But the peasants will not embrace such tasks if the leadership does not appear to present a genuine and less exploitative alternative than does the colonial system itself. They thus exercise a kind of passive veto over the movement and over those who lead it. Moreover, the establishment of participatory institutions throughout the liberated areas has enabled the peasant also to play an active role in helping to arbitrate the issue of the movement's direction. This fact became particularly important in 1968–69 when the contestation within FRELIMO's petty-bourgeois leadership—this group drawn initially from classes like those cited by Cabral with reference to Guinea—reached its boiling point. Then the progressive elements closest to the popular base of the struggle carried the day for their conception of the direction which the movement should take.

The popular base was significant. At the Congress of 1968 it was the delegates representing the people in the rural areas and those representing the army working inside the country who supported Mondlane; similarly, in 1969 when Simango broke with the movement, his defection found little or no echo in the liberated areas. It became clear that it was those who could work with the peasants as cadres—resolving in their own methods of political and educational work the contradiction between leadership and peasant participation —who had been able to consolidate their positions within the movement while others dropped by the wayside. It was also such cadres who could be expected to carry the revolution forward. For in the very process of this contestation the movement was encouraged to develop a new ideology, to move from "primitive nationalism," as Marcellino dos Santos has termed it, to revolutionary nationalism."

In short, the popular, peasant base of the struggle has become the key both to FRELIMO's military success and to its own internal clarity as a revolutionary movement. And this, in turn, has encouraged its cadres to return to the people with even more searching solutions for the problems of the peasantry: not merely genuine democratic involvement at village, circle, district, and regional levels, but also a comprehensive and practical program of socioeconomic transformation.

In our case the necessity to define a revolutionary ideology with greater precision emerged when we started to build the liberated areas, to engage ourselves in national reconstruction. As always, the task of building a society economically poses the problem of the type of production and distribution, and especially who is going to benefit from what the society produces. This life process also raises more sharply than in the classroom the deeper question of the type of ideology to embrace. So to summarize, there comes a stage when it becomes clear why everybody in the nation should accept the idea that the main aim of the struggle is to advance the interests of the working people. In the field or organizing the people we follow collectivistic ways as is the case, for example, with our cooperative movement in the liberated areas.

It is precisely here that peasants begin to be drawn "into the process of cooperative endeavor" (Alavi). The further radicalization of the nationalist movement, and the need to consolidate its rural base, create this kind of momentum. In the words of Samora Machel, FRELIMO's president:

we leaders, cadres, fighters and militants must work hard to make the masses adopt and live by the collective spirit, using collective methods of production, which will make it possible to enhance the spirit of collective living thereby increasing the sense of unity, discipline and organization. Adopting a collective consciousness in work means renouncing individualism and considering that all the cultivated plots belong to us, that all the granaries and houses are ours, the people's. It means that I must unite with others in a cooperative, a production brigade. We will cultivate, harvest and stand guard together, and together we will protect that which belongs not to me or you, but to us. The field is not mine or yours, but ours. The pupil in the school, the soldier in the base and the patient and the nurse in the hospital all have collective consciousness. No one looks upon the school, the base or the hospital as their private property, and everyone therefore

107

takes an enthusiastic interest in advancing the work in the school, base and hospital. As a result progress is made, the work advances and the enemy cannot so easily attack. Where there is collective spirit, we are more organized, there is better discipline and a proper division of labor. There is also more initiative, a greater degree of sacrifice and we learn more, produce more and fight better, with more determination.[37]

This step is in some ways more difficult than laying the initial bases of armed struggle. Joaquim Chissano of FRELIMO suspects that "peasants are generally rather conservative and you have to go step by step. In our case there are traditional ways of cooperation, such as mutual help, and at the first stage we encourage them. Later we establish district committees to administer the area, and groups within this framework to look after agriculture. In their discussions within these committees, little by little the members come to understand the benefits of working collectively."[38] In other words, given the quality of FRELIMO cadres and the general participative atmosphere in the liberated areas, striking results can be achieved. When, for example, I visited one village in Mozambique where this process had been underway for only a year or two, I discovered a division of labor that incorporated a significant proportion of collectively farmed fields, work on these being recorded in a logbook against eventual distribution of the proceeds. I found metalworkers and basketmakers who had originally worked as mini-entrepreneurs in the village, now working as part of this collective division of labor, their time spent also being recorded in the village book. Such dramatic developments may eventually inspire social scientists to write books like *Fanshen* about them; for the present we must rely on twentieth-century versions of travelers' tales. But the latter evidence is impressive and does begin to suggest that in such a peasantry, increasingly well-organized and now working self-consciously against various forms of exploitation, there can be seen some guarantee of the continued forward momentum of the Mozambican revolution, even after independence has been won. This is also the underlying thrust of Dos Santos's comment in a recent interview:

I accept that [communal effort] is partly made easier by the demands of war. But does that mean that once we have independence the approach will be changed? In the particular conditions of fighting against Portuguese colonialism, revolutionary attitudes are not only possible but necessary. If we do not follow collectivist attitudes we will not be able to face the enemy successfully. In this sense it is true to say that the internal dynamic of the struggle is such that the conditions generate collectivist thinking. But one should also say that even if the origins of such attitudes are partly pragmatic it can, nevertheless, provide a basis for the growth of real social revolution. There is certainly a strong possibility that in the course of the collectivist effort a situation is created from which it will be difficult to withdraw. If our organization maintains a true revolutionary leadership the special circumstances of the process of our liberation open up real possibilities for an advance from liberation to revolution.

How to make certain that this is achieved?

The main defense must be to popularize the revolutionary aims and to create such a situation that if for one reason or another at some future time some people start trying to change these aims, they will meet with resistence from the masses.

Tanzania

For Tanzania, the future is now. In consequence, that country reveals much more clearly some of the problems of peasant-based structural transformation. The absence of "tyranny and misery" of the proportions offered by Portuguese colonialism means that those features that tend to *divide* and to *differentiate* the peasantry become far more prominent aspects of the terrain of struggle than in Mozambique. At the same time, the leadership that has emerged in Tanzania has not been moved to cleanse and rededicate itself to anything like the extent of that in Mozambique. Despite the Arusha Declaration and *Mwongozo* (the TANU Guidelines of 1971), it is the more conservative wing of the petty-bourgeoisie which seems increasingly to be consolidating itself, with the result that the cadre-based methods of work that might serve to crystallize and focus peasant discontent and positive aspirations are not so well developed. From both points of view, Tanzania falls short; rather than a dialectic being established between leaders and led that reinforces forward movement, the gap between them seems to be growing.

Still, what is striking about Tanzania is that it can be discussed in these terms at all. In most of independent Africa the break between nationalist parties and peasantry was of a kind described by Fanon, often from a point even prior to the winning of independence. In Tanzania, on the other hand, an attempt has been made to resolve such a contradiction within the framework of the country's policy of "socialism and self-reliance." "Peasants" were to become, with "workers," a crucial agency for transforming established structures from within—for a "quiet revolution," in effect. I have traced elsewhere the background to this attempt, and some of its continuing strengths and weaknesses.[39] Here it is relevant to note three themes that have defined the rural dimensions of Tanzania's socialist project.

First, there has been President Nyerere's oft-repeated emphasis on the necessity that, territorially, the masses—"the workers and peasants"—become responsible for their own socialist development, distrusting their leaders and holding them firmly to account.[40] Though not always clearly defined in the language of class struggle, the point was thus being made that *the peasantry* has an interest in confronting those elements who might work to sustain its continued subordination.[41] Moreover, this aspiration found some reinforcement in subsequent policy initiatives. *Mwongozo* further called upon the people to check their leaders.[42] It is true that this invitation was, in the first instance, taken up most actively by the workers in the urban areas; nonetheless, *Mwongozo* confirmed the general emphasis upon the peasants' own positive role. And the whole process of decentralizing planning processes closer to the villages in 1971–73, however much disfigured in practice, was designed to redress a situation where "to the mass of the people, power is still something wielded by others." With decentralization, "more and more people must be trusted with responsibility—that is its whole purpose."[43]

Second, there has been a desire to pre-empt the further development of capitalist relations of production in the rural areas themselves:

as land becomes more scarce we shall find ourselves with a farmers' class and a laborers' class, with the latter being unable either to work for themselves or to receive a full return for the contribution they are making to total output. They will become a "rural proletariat" depending on the decisions of other men for their existence, and subject in consequence to all the subservience, social and economic inequality, and insecurity, which such a position involves.

Thus we still have in this country a predominantly peasant society in which farmers work for themselves and their families, and are helped and protected from exploitation by cooperative marketing arrangements [sic]. Yet the present trend is away from the extended family production and social unity, and toward the development of a class system. It is this kind of development which would be inconsistent with the growth of a socialist Tanzania in which all citizens could be assured of human dignity and equality, and in which all were able to have a decent and constantly improving life for themselves and their children.[44]

In this respect, too, socialism was seen as a way out of the peasant condition. By becoming "socialists" peasants would avoid the other possible fates discussed above—their continued subordination as a peasantry or their destruction under "the wave of (capitalist) progress." Third, there has been a desire to improve the quality of rural life by raising productivity and by slowly but surely making available necessary services and amenities. Implicit was an agreement with Raikes' formulation:

It has been shown time and time again that tremendous resources of productivity and creativity can be released in peasants and other producers once they take control of their own production process and control democratically its planning and implementation.[45]

The mechanism chosen to realize these goals has been the "ujamaa (socialist) village" policy—an attempt to structure collective agricultural communities at the base of the Tanzanian system that would give concrete expression to the peasants' involvement in the tasks of socialist construction. In working to build "rural socialism," peasants could be expected to transform themselves. Moreover, *ujamaa* communities, once established, could also be expected to provide more effective rallying points for critical action by an increasingly radicalized and organized peasantry, and hence the greater likelihood of a "real, rather than a theoretical, check upon the petty-bourgeoisie of party and bureaucracy, at local and national levels, by the mass of the population in the interests of socialist development."[46] And this on a nationwide scale. It is true that much of the original emphasis seemed to lie on the formation of brand-new villages in marginal-subsistence areas, but this was by no means an exclusive emphasis. Already, in the first major policy paper that launched the *ujamaa* approach, the president made clear that in established cash-cropping areas the move toward collectivism was equally to be fostered—even if, of necessity, by more subtle and graduated means:

> It must be accepted . . . that socialist progress in these areas will be more difficult to achieve, for when vacant land is not available there is only one way to create a community farm; that is by individual farmers coming together and joining their pieces of land and working them in common . . .
> It may be that the way to start under these circumstances is to operate first on the basis of working groups, but with the individual plots retained—that is, on the basis of mutual help. This would be simply a revival, and perhaps an extension, of the traditional system of joint activity, making it applicable to existing farms and not just to land clearing or house building. By working together on their private farms the farmers will be able to finish different jobs more quickly, or to do things which would be too difficult for any of them individually. They will then have time to do other useful things—either by themselves or cooperatively.
> This first step of mutual help can be followed by others. The farmers could buy certain essential goods cooperatively—things like fertilizers for example—or they could together build a store for their coffee, or something else which is of use to them all. By doing such things together the farmers will be gradually moving toward an acceptance of ujamaa socialism.[47]

Reference was also made in that paper to the peculiar problems of bringing collective agriculture to "animal husbandry" areas. In short, the initial formulation was not a crude one: it began with the firm recognition that Tanzania contained a markedly diverse range of peasantries.

The original guidelines for the policy seemed also to strongly emphasize peasant spontaneity as a key to progress. Thus Nyerere argued that "any citizen who understands the principles of ujamaa is encouraged to take the initiative"[48] and stressed again and again that the transition to collectivism was to be a voluntary one. Discussing his paper "Socialism and Rural Development," he noted that "it is directed to all the people of Tanzania—or at least all of those who live in the rural areas. It is an outline of a policy of inter-linked, self-governing village communities which are *of* the people, and which therefore cannot be created for them or imposed on them. The paper, therefore, calls for leadership, but not for orders to be given; it directs the people along the socialist path, but excludes any attempt to whip them into it—saying clearly that you cannot force people to lead socialist lives." But the call for "leadership" is equally crucial. Nyerere, in fact, sought the key to success in leaders who will be, arguably, those very *cadres* whose importance we discussed earlier, persons who "will lead by doing."[49] He specifies some of the methods of work of such people and concludes:

> The members of an ujamaa village must control their own affairs—
> I say it again! But the role of a leader is crucial and good leadership
> will make all the difference to the socialist success and the material
> success of such a community.

Spontaneity and leadership—with cadres who will resolve that contradiction! Let us again check both terms of that equation. In Tanzania, peasant protest was an active ingredient in the nationalist movement; moreover, the party (TANU) which gave a focus to nationalism was linked more closely to this peasant base than other such parties elsewhere in Africa. This was one factor that facilitated the forging of the progressive program of "socialism and self-reliance" by one wing of the territorial leadership in the postcolonial period. In addition, there have been some significant peasant actions subsequent to the winning of independence—not least the taking of a number of local initiatives to establish rural collectivization in

113

scattered parts of the country—notably in remote Ruvuma region. In the latter case, the Ruvuma Development Association (RDA., with its small attendant organization of cadres, the Social and Economic Revolutionary Army, SERA.) was established formally under the umbrella of TANU, but more spontaneously than that fact might tend to suggest. In important ways it became a prototype for Nyerere when he moved to generalize this and other "unofficial" experiments into a national "ujamaa villages" policy. Moreover, the potency of such rural collectives in institutionalizing a peasant challenge to class formation—in particular, a challenge to those whose power and privilege had begun to crystallize around the apparatuses of state and party—can be seen in the history of the RDA's struggles with the bureaucracy and with local notables over a number of years in Ruvuma. It can also be gauged from the fact that the RDA was dissolved by the party, possibly against the president's better judgment, in 1969.[50]

Despite the example of the RDA, it is nonetheless clear that "spontaneity" has been an inadequate source of rural transformation in Tanzania. A potential is there, but to trigger off peasant consciousness around a national program of socialist reconstruction and to give this program its local embodiment in collective units requires the sort of leadership identified by Nyerere. It could of course be argued that in the period after 1967, when Nyerere and his colleagues launched their overall project of transforming the economy and consolidating a progressive leadership, some of the preconditions for drawing peasants "into the process of cooperative endeavor" did exist.[51] Yet the inability of Tanzanian leaders to cope with the reality of a mobilized peasantry when it had sprung to life (as witness the RDA experience) is suggestive of a lingering problem. Not surprisingly, they have been equally unsuccessful in becoming active agents for mobilizing such a peasantry into existence and releasing its energies elsewhere in the country where this is necessary.[52] On balance, the trend toward the *bureaucratization* of the leadership (or, more accurately, its crystallization as a privileged class around the apparatus of the state) has begun to outpace any countertendency that would serve to transform it into a complement of socialist cadres.[53] Raikes argues that this degeneration has in turn determined a running down of the ujamaa policy into one marked by coercion, by the uneconomic and demobilizing reliance upon solely material incentives, and by compromise with the locally privileged who have most to lose from collectivization.

The consolidation of a more radical overall tendency there would, as in liberated Mozambique, have been reflected in more adequate methods of political work at the local level as well. For despite Nyerere's emphasis, cited above, on adapting the policy to suit the situation of diverse peasantries little has been done to follow up on this insight. Yet the need to generate detailed knowledge both of political stresses and strains at the local level, and of the realities of productive potential there, is at least as crucial to those engaged in facilitating the transition to collectivization in Tanzania as it is to those engaged in mobilizing a base for guerrilla warfare in Mozambique. If anything, it is even more important, for the range of variation of the "articulation of modes of production" is vast in Tanzania, while the necessity to give the struggle for socialism a concrete and meaningful expression at the local level is even more pressing in the absence of a direct physical threat to the peasantry like that provided by the Portuguese colonialists.

Several writers have addressed themselves to these realities; Woods discussing a range of "area-based peasantries" in Tanzania and Cliffe[54] pinpointing six different "broad types of rural situation" that need seperate consideration: highland high-density areas, medium-density cash-crop areas, marginal subsistence areas, frontier areas, settler/estate areas, pastoral and semipastoral areas. Furthermore, Cliffe, in a number of his writings, has spelled out some of the implications for socialist construction of this range of variation by identifying differing strategies for engaging the peasants of each such area in collective activity. He finds one key, particularly in advanced areas, in premising strategies upon the opportunities for struggle offered by class divisions internal to the areas themselves. In the absence of such strategies those peasants who have shifted furthest toward a capitalist posture may sieze the day, as in Bukoba where "in the contemporary period when the Tanzanian government is attempting to restructure the modes of production into cooperative forms in order to avoid class differentiation, the policy was preempted by a coalition of bureaucrats and the locally privileged. They translated the policy into terms which safeguarded the existing positions of rich and middle peasants by removing poor peasants who had little or no land to so-called 'ujamaa' villages in resettlement areas."

Nor is the latter case an isolated one. Raikes would see it merely as a further example of a more general phenomenon—the class alliance of bureaucrat and "kulak":

> Thus communal labor for ujamaa villages required communal landholding, something which required careful political education for peasants both large and small if they were to give of all or part of the private plots on which their livelihood depended. More particularly of course, the larger farmers plainly stood to lose, and this could have led to some difficult choices in view of their considerable local political influence. The discomfort would have been the greater since by training, inclination and previous practice, the administrators were accustomed to work through precisely these local leaders and specifically through "progressive" (i.e., large) farmers. This had been a stated objective of colonial agricultural policy, and was largely continued through the first six years of Independence. Concentration of advice, credit and membership of cooperative and other local committees upon such groups had led, in many areas (and especially the richer ones), to the emergence of fairly small and tight groups of relatively wealthy and influential peasants and capitalist farmers whose relations to government staff were much closer than those of the mass of the peasantry.[55]

Is there added steam to be drawn upon in such a situation? The work of the Iringa Regional Commissioner, Dr. Wilbert Klerru, in emphasizing class contradictions in the Ismani area, isolating the "kulaks," taking over holdings, and releasing the energies of poor and middle peasant strata might seem to suggest so, though in the event it lead to Klerru himself being assassinated by a "rich peasant."[56] And Ismani is a frontier area where capitalist relations are the most fully developed in Tanzania and the least muted by quasi-traditional identifications and solidarities. Where "middle peasants" are a more dominant proportion of the rural population than in Ismani, the precise blend of class struggle, exemplification of collectivity, and technical innovation to be encouraged would have to be a more nuanced one.[57] Of the need for such effective and militant local strategies, however, there can be no doubt.

But, to repeat, the "methods of work" that might generate such strategies have not been forthcoming. The one effort, in 1967, to develop, systematically, a core of cadres who could be expected genuinely to release peasant energies around the promise of collective action floundered on the reef of bureaucratic and political hostility to such a program.[58] Instead, quite dubious alternative policies have been mounted, some of which have already been mentioned: a "frontal approach" directed by civil servants (generally themselves from more developed regions) toward backward areas least able to defend themselves and reduced in content to mere "villagization," rather than collective enterprise; a ceding of other "ujamaa" experiments (in tea and tobacco) to the purview of World Bank experts little concerned to guarantee socialist relations of production; and so on. Meanwhile, amid the degeneration of his policy, President Nyerere seems to have become more shrill and desperate in an attempt to recover the ground that has been lost. His latest utterance on the subject has struck a particularly uncharacteristic note: "To live in villages is an order," in the words of a *Daily News, Tanzania* headline.

President Nyerere said yesterday that living together in villages is now an order. And it should be implemented in the next three years. This was a Tanu decision. And any leader who hesitated to implement it would not be tolerated because he would be retarding national development. Addressing a public rally at Endabashi, Mbulu District, Mwalimu [i.e., Nyerere] said there was a need for every Tanzanian to change his mode of life if rapid progress was to be achieved. People who refuse to accept development changes were stupid, if not ignorant and stubborn.[59]

There may be more promising countertendencies at the base of the system, though (as noted elsewhere) it is workers and students who have thus far responded most actively to *Mwongozo*'s invitation to take power into their own hands.[60] Nonetheless, in a country so rurally biased as Tanzania it remains true, ultimately, that "the only available class *base* for revolutionary transformation would seem to be a reconstructed peasantry—even if elements from other strata of society provide much of the leadership."[61] Nor is it likely that the peasantry has been entirely unaffected by the experience of struggle over the direction postcolonial Tanzania will take. Difficult though it is to gauge, some measure of consciousness-raising has undoubtedly taken place in the rural areas, even if the ujamaa program has yet to give it effective institutional expression. Indeed, Von Freyhold seems to argue that the advance has been substantial, though seriously flawed:

> While society has changed, parts of the bureaucracy have not yet fully understood that the peasants have emerged victorious from colonial domination. The old vices of bureaucracy—commandism, hasty decisions without investigation, red-tape and superiority feelings—have survived and it will probably take a cultural revolution—including communal re-education through self-criticism—to readapt the superstructure to its new social base.[62]

Whence such a cultural revolution? In Handeni, Von Freyhold does see seeds of growing consciousness even in the rather compromised villages that have emerged from implementation of the ujamaa policy there. Furthermore, she feels that the struggle to determine the overall direction of the system is still sufficiently alive to make the opting for a cadre-based strategy—and a consequent strengthening of a rejuvenated party over and against the "staff" or bureaucracy —a continuing possibility. This conclusion is controversial—some would argue that it is the bureaucrats and not the peasants who have emerged victorious—but her perception as to the need "to change the structures of communication between the villages and the outside (in a way) which could bring more knowledge, more motivation and more self-assurance to the common members of the villages" is much less controversial. In the end she returns to familiar recommendations, recommendations that recall the dynamic of developments witnessed in Mozambique:

118

The kind of recruitment, training and task-description needed for political cadres will in any case have to change as the party and the peasants gain more experience with each other and with ujamaa. What matters at the moment is that the necessity of cadres [should be] realized and that different ways of finding and educating the right kind of people be tried. Strengthening the party at its base would have to be a priority not only because peasants need political guidance but also because the party at higher levels cannot grow into a meaningful institution without confrontation with the real and concrete problems on the ground.[63]

Here would be a rejoining of the dialectic between leadership and peasantry that we have seen to be so important. Time alone will tell whether Tanzania still retains the capacity to reverse all those trends that suggest the running-down of its socialist experiment and whether it can begin again to consolidate a peasant base for itself along the lines thus suggested.[64]

The two cases that we have discussed are important, but they are not entirely typical of the continent as a whole. Southern Africa is crucial in its own right; moreover, successful revolution in Mozambique (using the term "revolution" in its broadest sense to include a successful challenge both to colonialism and to any prospect of subsequent neocolonialism) would also be a stimulus to developments in the rest of Africa. But, as we have seen, the colonial factor —Portuguese "ultra-colonialism"—has given a point and purpose to nationalism there that has fashioned it, ineluctably and in the preindependence period, into a revolutionary ideology and a revolutionary movement—of peasants. Tanzania, though already an independent state, is also atypical in that some attempt has been made *by those already in positions of authority* to mobilize the peasants (and workers) to support, even to demand, radical structural transformation.

With reference to Tanzania, there are those who would suggest that a point has now been reached that demands a more root-and-branch, from-the-bottom-up, challenge to established structures, and who argue, in effect, that a much less ambiguous revolutionary thrust is becoming a necessity there.[65] Whatever the answer to this difficult question, the fact remains that the situation elsewhere in independent (and neocolonized) Africa is far less ambiguous and the imperative of such a straightforward challenge to established authority more clear-cut if the peasant's plight is to be alleviated. There the time has arrived when "someone" operating outside the established structures must attempt again to convince the peasantry, in Nyerere's phrase, "that their own efforts can lead to an improvement in their lives!" Of course, a further exploration of this prospect is not our concern here. Yet if and when mass-based revolutions do become a more characteristic feature of other parts of Africa, there will be lessons, both positive and negative, to be learned by African revolutionaries from the experience of Mozambique and Tanzania—lessons about the precise range of peasantries that exist in Africa and, most important, about the methods that might facilitate these peasantries making the revolution their own. We have begun to touch upon some of these lessons in this paper. More generally, it has become obvious that additional scientific work on the question of African peasantries can be expected to make a positive contribution to the revolutionary process on the continent.

NOTES

1. Karl Marx, "The Eighteenth Brumaire of Louis Bonaparte," in Marx, *Survey from Exile* (Harmondsworth, 1973), p. 239.

2. Nigel Harris, "The Revolutionary Role of the Peasants," *International Socialism*, No. 41, London, Dec.-Jan. 1969–70.

3. Malcolm Caldwell, "The Revolutionary Role of the Peasants—2," ibid.

4. Quoted in Daniel Singer, *Prelude to Revolution* (New York, 1970), p. 1.

5. See Paul Sweezy's particularly strong statement of this point in his "Workers and the Third World" in George Fischer (ed.), *The Revival of American Socialism* (New York, 1971), p. 168: "If we consider capitalism as a global system, which is the only correct procedure, we see that it is divided into a handful of exploiting countries and a much more numerous and populous group of exploited countries. The masses in these exploited dependencies constitute a force in the global capitalist system which is revolutionary in the same sense and for the same reasons that Marx considered the proletariat of the early period of modern industry to be revolutionary. And finally, world history since the Second World War proves that this revolutionary force is really capable of waging successful revolutionary struggles against capitalist domination."

6. Eric Wolf, *Peasant Wars of the Twentieth Century* (New York, 1969), p. 276.

7. Lionel Cliffe, "Rural Class Formation in East Africa," paper presented to the "Peasant Seminar" of the Centre of International and Area Studies, University of London, 23 Nov. 1973, p. 1.

8. Hamza Alavi, "Peasants and Revolution," in Ralph Miliband and John Saville (eds.), *The Socialist Register 1965* (London, 1965).

9. Alavi's emphasis suggests an additional point of crucial relevance to our discussion of Africa: that "the peasantry" is not uniform. Alavi's own distinction between "poor" and "middle" peasant is one of a number of possible differentiations to be made among various peasantries in any specific historical setting.

10. Mark Selden, "People's War in China and Vietnam" in Lawrence Kaplan (ed.), *Revolutions: A Comparative Study* (New York, 1973), pp. 374–75.

11. L. A. Fallers, "Are African Cultivators to be Called 'Peasants'?," *Current Anthropology*, No. 2, 1961, pp. 108–10.

12. See William Derman, "Peasants: The Africa Exception?," *American Anthropologist*, No. 74, 1972, pp. 779–82.

13. John S. Saul and Roger Woods, "Africa Peasantries," in Teodor Shanin (ed.), *Peasants and Peasant Societies* (Harmondsworth, 1971).

14. For a general overview of this process, see Walter Rodney, *How Europe Underdeveloped Africa* (London and Dar es Salaam, 1972).

15. Ken Post, *On "Peasantisation" and Rural Class Differentiation in Western Africa*, ISS Occasional Papers (The Hague, 1970).

16. William Derman in his book, *Serfs, Peasants and Socialists* (Berkeley/London, 1973), suggests, following Wolf, a very broad definition of "rent" to encompass these varying realities while maintaining conformity with certain of the literature on peasantries on other continents.

17. Colin Leys, "Politics in Kenya: The Development of Peasant Society," *British Journal of Political Science*, I 1970, p. 326.

18. Barrington Moore, *Social Origins of Dictatorship and Democracy: Lord and Peasant in the Making of the Modern World* (Boston, 1966), p. 505.

19. This fact also demonstrates the urgency of a peasant-based revolution in Africa, for peripheral capitalism seems unlikely, by its further evolution, to produce an alternative agency, a fully developed proletariat, which could underwrite a socialist way out of the dead-end of underdevelopment.

20. Cf. Frantz Fanon, *The Wretched of the Earth* (Harmondsworth, 1967).

21. Amilcar Cabral, "Brief Analysis of the Social Structure in Guinea," in his *Revolution in Guinea* (London, 1969). On page 50 he draws an explicit comparison with the Chinese case: "The conditions of the peasantry in China were very different: the peasantry had tradition of revolt, but this was not the case in Guinea, and so it was not possible for our party militants and propaganda workers to find the same kind of welcome among the peasantry of Guinea for the idea of national liberation as the idea found in China."

22. The "crisis of feudalism," which is often attendant upon the incursion of capitalism and which intensifies a number of contradictions for the peasantry, will not, therefore, be so prominent a feature.

23. See the analysis in my essay *The Dialectic of Tribe and Class in Kenya and Uganda*, forthcoming.

24. Martin Kilson, *Political Change in a West Africa State*, among others.

25. Julius K. Nyerere, "Introduction," *Freedom and Socialism* (London and Dar es Salaam, 1968), p. 29.

26. Jules Gerard-Libois, "The New Class and Rebellion in the Congo," in Miliband and Saville, *The Socialist Register 1966* (London, 1966). Gerard-Libois goes on to note, significantly, that "the rebellion did not find the united, effective and revolutionary organization it required, and it is very doubtful whether the brief experience of the People's Republic made any contribution to its creation," p. 278.

27. Moreover, it is also obvious that trends in the urban areas (the activities of workers and/or lumpen elements, for example) will be important in determining the nature and extent of peasant involvement in movements directed toward radical social reconstruction.

28. Julius K. Nyerere quoted in *The Nationalist,* Dar es Salaam, 5 Sept. 1967, and cited in John S. Saul, "African Socialism in One Country: Tanzania" in G. Arrighi and J. S. Saul, *Essays on the Political Economy of Africa* (New York, 1973), p. 248.

29. This distinction is developed, with reference to an advanced capitalist setting, in Andre Gorz, *Socialism and Revolution* (New York, 1973).

30. Eduardo Mondlane, *The Struggle for Mozambique* (Harmondsworth, 1969), p. 116.

31. "FRELIMO Faces the Future," an interview by Joe Slovo with Marcelino dos Santos in *The African Communist,* No. 55, 1973, p. 29.

32. In Perry Anderson, "Portugal and the End of Ultra Colonialism," *New Left Review,* nos. 16, 17, 18, 1962.

33. For a brief account of my initial impressions, see the article "Lesson in Revolution for a Canadian Lecturer" in *Mozambique Revolution,* No. 52, July-Sept. 1972.

34. See also Jorge Rebelo's comment on the struggle in the province of Manica e Sofala: "One of the most interesting developments in Manica e Sofala has been the response of the people, which has been even stronger than that in Tete, again, we believe, because of the experience of oppression which the people here have." (In "Comrade Rebelo's Report to CFM on Current Developments in Mozambique, June 19th, 1973," in *Committee for a Free Mozambique News and Notes,* (New York, 1973).

35. Don Barnett, *Peasant Types and Revolutionary Potential in Colonial Africa* (Richmond, B.C., 1973).

36. John S. Saul, "FRELIMO and the Mozambique Revolution" in Arrighi and Saul, *op cit.,* chap. 8.

37. Samora Machel, "Sowing the Seeds of Liberation," in *Mozambique Revolution*, No. 49, Oct.-Dec. 1971, pp. 23–4.

38. "Chissano: within 5 years the liberated areas will be developed 10 times more than under colonialism," interview with Joaquim Chissano in *Ceres*, Rome, July-Aug. 1973, p. 40.

39. John S. Saul, "African Socialism in One Country: Tanzania," op. cit.

40. Thus "President Nyerere has called on the people of Tanzania to have great confidence in themselves and safeguard the nation's hard-won freedom. He has warned the people against pinning all their hopes on the leadership who are apt to sell the people's freedom to meet their lusts. Mwalimu (i.e., Nyerere) warned that the people should not allow their freedom to be pawned as most of the leaders were purchaseable. He warned further that in running the affairs of the nation the people should not look on their leaders as 'saints or prophets.' The President stated that the attainment of freedom in many cases resulted merely in the change of colours, white to black faces without ending exploitation and injustices, and above all without the betterment of the life of the masses." This statement is from the newspaper account cited in note 28.

41. This includes some attack upon imperialism—the confrontation with the "new class" of leaders/bureaucrats is implicitly this throughout, and a wide-ranging program of nationalizations and self-reliance is part of Tanzania's broader socialist policy. Nonetheless, it seems fair to argue that the overall policy has not been sufficiently clear concerning the peasants' role in subordination to international capitalism—especially vis-à-vis the world market system. Strategies for the rural sector have been weak in linking peasant production to a new pattern of demand brought into existence by structural change in the industrial-/urban sector, the latter in turn to be facilitated by a more decisive break with dependency. Cf. Saul, op. cit. (see note 28), for a more detailed critique along these lines.

42. *Mwongozo/The TANU Guidelines* (Dar es Salaam, 1971).

43. Julius K. Nyerere, *"Decentralisation" in Freedom and Development* (Dar es Salaam and London, 1973), p. 347. Nyerere adds that "those who cause the new system to become enmeshed in bureaucratic procedures will, as they are discovered, be treated as what they are—saboteurs."

44. Julius K. Nyerere, "Socialism and Rural Development," in his *Freedom and Socialism, op. cit.* This is an important perception of trends in rural Tanzania, though Roger Woods, in his "Peasants and Peasantries in Tanzania and their Role in Socio-Political Development" [in Rural Development Research Committee, *Rural Co-operation in Tanzania*

(Dar es Salaam, 1974)] argues that involution and stagnation may be an equally prominent feature in many such areas.

45. Philip Raikes, "Ujamaa Vijijini and Rural Socialist Development," *Review of African Political Economy,* No. 3, 1975.

46. John S. Saul, "Who is the Immediate Enemy?" in Cliffe and Saul (eds.), *op. cit.,* vol. 2, p. 357.

47. Nyerere, "Socialism and Rural Development," op. cit., pp. 361–62.

48. Nyerere, "After the Arusha Declaration," in *Freedom and Socialism,* op. cit.

49. Nyerere, "Implementation of Rural Socialism," in *Freedom and Development.*

50. R. Ibbott, "The Disbanding of the Rubuma Development Association, Tanzania," London, Nov. 1969.

51. For example, "leaders" were sealed off from very gross "conflicts of interests" vis-à-vis the private sector under the terms of the 1967 Leadership Code (although familial links to "kulaks" often remained); moreover, given the stated attempt to undermine elite consolidation and to rally the masses as "workers and peasants," the instrumentalization of the peasants by manipulating tribalism has been significantly reduced, thus encouraging the latter to come into more direct, unmediated, confrontation with structural realities.

52. See Raikes, op. cit.; Michaela von Freyhold, "The Government Staff and Ujamaa Villages," paper presented to the Annual Social Science Conference of the University of East Africa, Dar es Salaam, Dec. 1973; Lionel Cliffe, "Planning Rural Development" in Uchumi Editorial Board, *Towards Socialist Planning, Tanzanian Studies* (Dar es Salaam, 1972). For example, as I have argued on p. 292 in my "African Socialism in One Country: Tanzania," it is . . . in the rural areas that manifestations of the hectoring, bureaucratic style of such a leadership are most likely to have the predicted effect of demobilizing the mass of the population, thus choking off that release of popular energies which is the program's ostensible aim."

53. The strongest statement of this position which, in fact, sees the leadership as compromised from the outset as a "bureaucratic bourgeoisie" is to be found in Issa Shivji, *Tanzania: The Class Struggle Continues* (Dar es Salaam, 1973); I have argued the existence of a struggle within the petty-bourgeoisie over the direction of Tanzanian development, a struggle which nonetheless evidences the growing strength of conservative elements, in "The State in Post-Colonial Societies: Tanzania," *Socialist Register* 1975, London.

54. Lionel Cliffe, "The Policy of Ujamaa Vijijini in the Class Struggle in Tanzania," in Lionel Cliffe and John S. Saul eds., *Socialism in Tanzania,* op. cit. vol. 2.

55. Raikes, op. cit. Von Freyhold, op. cit., even argues that kulaks can sometimes operate within so-called ujamaa villages to advance their interests, a point which is also developed in an interesting case study by H. U. E. Thoden van Velzen in his essay "A Case Study of Ujamaa Farming in Rungwe," in Rural Development Research Committee, *Rural Co-operation in Tanzania,* op. cit.

56. For an excellent, detailed account of developments in Ismani, see Adhu Awiti, "Class Struggle in Rural Society of Tanzania," *Maji Maji* Special Publication No. 7, Dar es Salaam, Oct. 1972.

57. Some examples of such possible strategies are presented in the final section of Rural Development Research Committee, op. cit., where both the alteration of relations of production and the expansion of productive forces are equally stressed in exploring the promise of rural collectivization.

58. See the account of this episode in N. Kisenge, "The Party in Tanzania," *Maji Maji* (Dar es Salaam, Sept. 1971).

59. *Daily News of Tanzania,* Nov. 7, 1973.

60. On the recent dramatic rise of worker activism, see Henry Mapolu, "The Workers' Movement in Tanzania," *Maji Maji,* no. 12, (Dar es Salaam, Sept. 1973), and Mapolu, "Labour unrest: irresponsibility or worker revolution?," *Jenga,* no. 12 (Dar es Salaam, 1972). For an attempt to theorize student unrest see Karim Hirji, "School Education and Underdevelopment in Tanzania," *Maji Maji,* no. 12, op. cit.

61. Cliffe, "The Policy of Ujamaa Vijijini and the Class Struggle in Tanzania," op. cit., p. 197.

62. Von Freyhold, op. cit. This is of a piece with my earlier conclusion which, however, now may seem excessively sanguine in light of the analyses by Raikes and others: "The horizon of really dramatic, cumulative change remains a distant one, but there can be little doubt that in the rural areas the *ujamaa* policy has given a content and structure to the struggle for progress in a nonrevolutionary situation around which consciousness can crystallize and a popular base may form" (in my "African Socialism in One Country," op. cit.).

63. Von Freyhold, op. cit. Von Freyhold sees this as a step toward facilitating the emergence of "peasant-experts" from within the village who would carry the process of transformation further; presumably, these kind of village activists would be precisely those militants who would

also feed into the party from the base, helping to transform it from within.

64. Unfortunately, there is little comparative material to go on, since many aspects of the Tanzanian situation are unique on the continent; moreover, despite its title and despite its many other virtues, Derman's book, *Serf's Peasants and Socialists,* does not take us far in understanding processes in Guiné which might conceivably be comparable, beyond his concluding sentence: "In my view, the transformation of peasants into socialists will be far more difficult than the transformation of serfs into peasants or the transformation of Guiné from colony to independent nation."

65. This might seem to be a conclusion to be drawn from Shivji's essay for example.

Landless Laborers and the Chicano Movement in

South Texas

JOHN SHOCKLEY*

Introduction

THOSE OF US WHO STUDY AMERICAN POLITICS ARE NOT USED TO thinking in terms of peasants. In fact if you ask an American about peasants, he is likely to think of China or Latin America, not of his own country. Depending upon how narrowly one defines the term *peasant,* such thinking may be justified. If, for example, we take a definition such as that used by Eric Wolf, who has argued that peasants are those who are "involved in cultivation and make autonomous decisions regarding the processes of cultivation," and who are more interested in sustenance for the family than in participation fully in the market, then the United States does not have many peasants.[1] But if we define the term to include those who have undergone the transformation from peasantry into agricultural proletarians, such as those who do not own the land but who work it for wages—as landless laborers, then we can indeed find remnants of a peasantry in the United States, particularly in certain parts of the country.

In this article I will be looking at an area of the country where landless laborers are common, and where the classification as land-

*For this paper I wish to express my gratitude to all those who helped me on my initial research in South Texas in 1970 and 1971, as well as to Arthur Rubel and Joseph Spielberg of Michigan State University and James Scott of the University of Wisconsin for their careful reading and comments on an earlier draft of this paper. Larry Carbaugh of the U.S. Bureau of the Census, Robert McElroy of the U.S. Department of Agriculture, and Conoley Kemper of the Good Neighbor Commission of Texas all helped in supplying me with some of the more recent data included in the paper.

less laborer almost always implies a racial or ethnic distinction that sets these people apart from the dominant whites in American society. This area is the southern portion of Texas, where hundreds of thousands of people of Mexican origin, and often of peasant background, now live. In looking at this area and these people, I will examine the growth of an independent Chicano political movement in Texas, and in particular, the extent to which landless laborers have been a force in this movement.

South Texas and the Chicano Movement

A majority of the people who live in South Texas are Mexican Americans, or Chicanos. In fact, about fifteen of the approximately twenty-five counties that comprise South Texas are at least three-quarters Chicano, and in nearly all the remaining ten counties Chicanos are a majority of the population. Overall, this area is one of the most poverty-stricken in America. There exists, however, more diversity than at first meets the eye, and this diversity seems to be crucial in terms of political mobilization and radicalization of the Chicano majority in the area.

Although in parts of South Texas Mexican-American settlement preceded Anglo-American settlement, now most Mexican Americans in South Texas are the result of massive migrations that began around the turn of the century, stimulated by the pressures of the Mexican Revolution and the Mexican economy. Most of these people did not participate in organized political activity in Texas at all. Those who did participate tended to be controlled by bosses, either Anglo or Mexican-American. With the growth of a middle class among Mexican Americans, particularly in the cities, self-help societies and political organizations began to form to press for equality and an end to discrimination.[2] These organizations were moderate to liberal in tone, and stressed the need for Mexican Americans to be responsible American citizens. An alternative to these two types of political activity—the patron-peon kind and the middle-class assimilationist kind—did not develop until the last decade, with the beginning of the Chicano movement.

The growth of self-consciousness and restiveness among Mexican

Americans, many of whom now preferred to be called Chicanos, occurred most noticeably in the 1960s, when the nation as a whole was experiencing political turmoil and Chicanos were being influenced by the Black movement. Like Blacks, Chicanos—especially younger and better educated ones—began to spurn the goals of integration and acculturation into Anglo-American society, and to push instead for the recovery and protection of their own identity. Anglos, rather than being models of respect and emulation, came to be considered "imperialists" and "gringos" who had taken away their land and were seeking to prevent Chicanos from becoming "masters of their own destiny." This attitude was not expressed in a coherent political manner in South Texas until the creation in the late 1960s of La Raza Unida, a Chicano political party set to do battle with Democrats and Republicans.

In previous years measuring the degree of mass political identification with the Chicano movement across South Texas was difficult. Not only did each locale need to be examined on the basis of the number of Mexican Americans elected to office, but the kinds of Mexican Americans elected needed to be examined to determine how much, if at all, they identified with the goals of the Chicano movement. Because of the decision by La Raza Unida to contest statewide offices in 1972, however, there now exist comparable figures across the state measuring the degree of support shown for the Chicano political party. An examination of these voting data immediately reveals the diversity we mentioned earlier. The percentage of Mexican Americans across South Texas on a county-by-county basis is no real predictor of the degree of support shown for the Chicano political party. Among the fourteen counties in South Texas with the largest percentage of Mexican Americans (ranging from ninety-eight percent to just over seventy-five percent), support for the party's gubernatorial and senatorial candidates fluctuated between just over fifty percent down to only one percent. Something more is necessary for the development of political support for an independent, left-wing Chicano political challenge to Anglo rule in Texas. The search for this something more constitutes the crux of this paper.

As a start to determining this, I have concentrated on the area where La Raza Unida has been most successful—the town of Crystal City, Texas, county seat of Zavala County. In examining the growth of the Chicano movement there, it is my hope that features about the town as it has experienced the movement will lead us to factors that are either necessary or important to the growth of this left-wing Chicano challenge to the current political set-up.

Looking at Crystal City, which has in many ways been the base of the Chicano revolt in South Texas, aspects of employment and the relationship of Chicanos to the land seem to be key factors in the success of the Chicano movement there. Several of these make the town more unusual than common in South Texas. In the first place, the town would never have been founded had it not been for the switch from ranching to agriculture that began in this area of South Texas around the turn of the century. The city was created out of a large ranch after the discovery that artesian water made irrigated farming profitable. This switch from ranching to farming required much labor, as brush had to be cleared and the vegetable crops tended. For this labor the Anglos looked to Mexicans across the border, who formed a nearly inexhaustible supply of cheap labor.[3] These Mexicans were eager for employment of any kind, and hard, backbreaking labor in the fields was something they would do. Anglos who owned the land and who made the decisions about converting the land from ranching to irrigated farming thus encouraged Mexicans to come. As one Anglo official expressed it to me, "All Crystal City was ever intended to be was a labor camp!"

Mexican Americans made up eighty percent or more of the town's population, and most of them were landless laborers. The overwhelming uniformity of the Mexican American population of the town was confirmed in a Works Progress Administration study in the late 1930s, which indicated that over ninety percent of the Mexican-American families in the city were farm laborers at least part of the year. Harsh economic realities confronted these people. Because the farm crop consisted only of cool-season vegetables that were planted and grown solely in the winter months, most of Crystal City's Mexican population had to become migrants in order to find

131

work during the late spring, summer, and early autumn. Emphasizing this point, the same WPA study indicated that over ninety percent of Crystal City's Mexican Americans were engaged in migrant labor.

This background has made Crystal City unusual in several respects. The "labor camp" base made Crystal City more heavily Mexican-American than is common even for South Texas. There are other communities in South Texas where such a high concentration of Mexican Americans can be found, such as Laredo, Eagle Pass, and Brownsville, but these towns have generally had a far more heterogeneous Mexican-American population. They have tended to be older communities, mainly situated on the border, with at least a few well-established, upper-class "Spanish" families who have always played an important role in community affairs. Crystal City, however, is more similar to certain towns in the Rio Grande Valley— such as Harlingen, McAllen, Edinburg, Pharr, and Weslaco—where the movement to farming likewise created new towns that were heavily populated by farm laborers from Mexico. Because of this background Crystal City was dominated from the very beginning by Anglos who had no need to compromise with older, established Mexican-American families.

Given these conditions, race lines in the community were class lines as well. Mexicans did the manual labor. Anglos owned the land and made the money. Although this general practice was not usual for South Texas, the degree to which race lines became class lines made Crystal City again somewhat unusual. It no doubt had a great deal to do with the issue of race eventually becoming the dominant question in politics once Mexican Americans in the town were organized.

In migrating, Crystal City Mexican Americans began to encounter different experiences and different ways of being treated from those they had encountered in South Texas. In particular, they tended to earn higher wages and meet with less racial discrimination when they worked in the North.[4] Being gone from Crystal City during much of the year and earning wages elsewhere, they were less susceptible to Anglo pressure than if they had lived permanently on the land of a particular patron. It was more difficult for the Anglos to attempt to control them or to embue them with the values of a patron-peon system.

These factors made Crystal City different from most other communities in South Texas, but the situation was not explosive so long as the Mexicans did not think of themselves as people able to challenge Anglo political control. This attitude of noninvolvement in community affairs was, however, gradually being eroded, and the erosion process was furthered by the establishment after World War II of a large Del Monte cannery plant. The plant, which by its very magnitude centralized much of the vegetable growing in the area, employed during the peak of the season more than a thousand workers. Most of them were seasonal workers, but some worked throughout the year. In addition to providing much-needed employment for the area, the plant was California-owned, and thus was subject to some ideas uncommon to South Texas. The most surprising of these was the plant's decision to allow unionization, since all their other plants were unionized. By 1956 a small Teamsters union was established at the plant and was recognized without any friction by the company.

The decision by Del Monte to move into Crystal City and establish a large plant, although welcomed in the beginning by many in the city's agricultural and business establishment, ultimately weakened these local Anglos' ability to control the situation. Having a large-scale plant employing hundreds of workers, paying wages not common for the area, and then allowing the workers the opportunity to unionize set Crystal City off even further from other South Texas communities.

Although the majority of the population continued to be landless laborers, the year-round workers at the Del Monte plant had become permanent residents, and by the early 1960s a small but growing Mexican-American middle class had developed that had a few organizations of its own. This group was beginning to be consulted by the Anglos on some matters. But the Mexican middle class was small and, owing to the history of the community, it was still quite fragile. Neither the Anglos nor the great majority of Mexican Americans themselves looked to this group for leadership.

133

It is not my purpose here to go into a detailed description of the Chicano political revolts that have rocked this community over the last decade.[5] I will for reasons of clarity, however, mention certain central features. Both revolts involved mobilizing the Mexican Americans of the community to attack a broad range of economic, social, and political inequalities Chicanos faced under Anglo domination, using electoral politics as a necessary tool for their success.[6]

The first revolt, begun in 1962–63 and defeated in 1965, was based on the Teamsters union at the Del Monte cannery. In overcoming the traditional political structure, outside political assistance and organization seems to have been crucial, and the Teamsters union supplied the link to that assistance. Acting as a shield to protect and promote Mexican-American political activity, they mobilized the cannery workers and the migrants of the community while preventing more massive retaliation by the Anglos. By a narrow margin its five Mexican-American candidates were swept into control of the city government on the basis of lower class, migrant workers support. This victory stunned the Anglo community and subsequently received national publicity. A group of poor, uneducated cannery men, former migrant workers, and marginal entrepreneurs found themselves in control of a town that had always been run by Anglos. The Mexican-American city government encountered intense resistance, was baffled by many of the legal complexities of government, and was defeated for re-election two years later when the Anglos regrouped and ran a slate including several from the new Mexican-American middle class.

For four years this Anglo, middle-class Mexican coalition ran Crystal City, and it looked like the Chicano activists, based on the workers at the plant and the town's migrant laborers, would never again rule. But in 1969 trouble flared up in the school system over discrimination against Mexican Americans. Led by José Angel Gutiérrez, a local boy who had gone on to receive graduate training in political science, Chicano activists of La Raza Unida organized the unrest, and broadened it to include basic questions that were loaded with emotional, symbolic, and substantive import about the way Anglos dominated Chicanos. This culminated in a massive school strike. The strike ended in Anglo capitulation to nearly all the

Chicano demands for bilingual and bicultural education, greater power to the student body, and the firing of several Anglo teachers. Following up the school victory, La Raza Unida organized the parents of the striking students into a broad-based, multifunctional community organization. Using this organization, they ran candidates for the city council and school board and, in a situation of intense electoral conflict and mobilization, took over control of the city government and school administration. Accompanied by much rhetoric and symbolism, the Chicano activists made massive changes in personnel in both the city and the school system, sought new sources of aid, undertook economic boycotts to try to intimidate or limit the strength of Anglo economic power in the area, and in general reoriented both structures toward greater concern for the Chicano workers and landless laborers.[7]

Using a strategy reminiscent of Saul Alinsky, La Raza Unida gained control of the city and the schools, and has been governing both for the last four years. No end of their control is in sight. Virtually all the Anglos have taken their children from the school system, and many have left the community altogether. Amidst rhetoric that proclaims the regeneration of the Chicano people and the defeat of the "gringo racists," the community is now more heavily Chicano than ever. Currently the Chicano activists are mobilizing for an attempt to gain control of the county government as well. La Raza Unida won some county offices, including the crucial position of sheriff, in 1972, but the Anglos still retain a number of county positions. The county government has in short proved much more difficult to take over, for reasons that seem to relate to the movement's very success in Crystal City.

This, then, is a brief summary of the political turmoil that has swept the community, and we return now to the question of how and why this has happened. What has made Crystal City the spearhead of the Chicano movement, and what role do landless laborers seem to have played in the struggle?

The Basis for the Chicano Mobilization

Calling upon historical factors we have already mentioned, observations of the rhetoric and programs of the Chicano government, and limited electoral analysis, I will attempt to answer this question.

At the time of the political revolts, the city's population was roughly eighty-five percent Mexican American, and of this over half were migrant workers during the summer months.[8] This gave Crystal City the highest proportion of migrants of any town in the state. In both revolts the migrant workers seem to have been the primary base of support, but in neither revolt were they the leadership. In the 1963 revolt, as we noted, the Teamsters union at the Del Monte cannery supplied the muscle, and the mayor was the Teamsters' business agent, a full-time cannery worker although himself a former migrant. The second revolt was lead by Chicano activists and intellectuals— again, not migrants.

Precinct returns do not allow us to measure migrant strength accurately because the city has too few precincts to be very helpful in measuring aggregate demographic bases of support.[9] My argument for the importance of the migrant worker base in the revolts stems from several other factors. In interviews in the city, many Anglos mentioned the "rabble" that had been mobilized in the revolts. Very often, "rabble" was used to mean the migrant workers, as opposed to the full-time, year-round, "responsible" Mexican-American elements of the community. A former mayor of Crystal City, himself a Mexican American who was labeled a "sell-out" and defeated by the Chicano activists, commented to me that Crystal City would be a very different place if it were not the home of so many migrants.

In addition, the Chicano activists themselves have directed much of their effort at mobilizing the migrants. Rallies were frequently held at "La Placita," an impoverished migrant worker section of the city. And changes in the school curricula, in particular those that reoriented the agricultural program from focusing upon concerns of farmers (which Anglo high school students had taken) to concerns of labor contracts, union organization, and migrant problems, have shown this interest in and concern for helping the migrants of the community.

Anglo calculations also seemed to indicate the importance of the migrants in the Chicano victories. This was clearly revealed by their desparate attempt, in the midst of the first Chicano government, to undercut the regime by initiating a recall petition and charter revision. This petition would have moved all city elections from April to July. If city elections had been held in July, with all the migrants gone, Anglos would have stood a much better chance of regaining control.

An election that ended in a tie vote, and forced a runoff election, seems further to indicate the role of the migrants in the Chicano victory. In the May primary election for the position of constable of one of the Crystal City precincts, an Anglo and a Chicano each received the same number of votes. But in the June runoff, occurring one month later and after many more migrants had left the community, the Anglo won easily. Both candidates received fewer votes in the runoff, but the Anglo's support was down by only six percent. The Chicano, however, lost over one third of his support, or six times as many supporters as the Anglo candidate had lost. This can be viewed as an indicator that migrants were voting overwhelmingly in support of the Chicano revolt.

Both Chicano revolts have drawn on the migrant base and the cannery workers, many of whom were seasonal employees and worked as migrants during the summer months. Arrayed against them have been virtually all the Anglos in the community, with their much greater political sophistication and experience, and those Mexican Americans in the community who for any of a number of reasons identified with Anglos or were repulsed by the Chicano leadership, its cultural and racial slogans, or its programs. Some of these were better-off Mexican Americans who were gaining acceptance in the Anglo community. Others were Mexican Americans who were susceptible to Anglo persuasion or pressure of one sort or another.

This dichotomy between pro- and anti-Chicano movement people helps explain in part why migrants have been the base of the movement, since migrants were lower-class people who were more isolated from Anglos than other Mexican Americans were. But a further distinction seems to shed more light on the role of migrants in the revolts. This distinction comes not from looking only at Crystal City, but from looking at the surrounding countryside as well.

The county in which Crystal City is located, Zavala County, has

Table 1

COMPARISON OF CITY AND SCHOOL DISTRICT SUPPORT FOR LA RAZA UNIDA

DATE	SCHOOL		CITY	DIFFERENCE BETWEEN SCHOOL DISTRICT AND CITY SUPPORT
1970	Raza Unida	1,344	1,341	
	Candidates	1,397	1,306	
		1,344		
	Average	1,362	1,323	39
	Anti-Raza	1,119	835	
	Unida	1,090	820	
	Candidates	1,081		
	Average	1,097	828	269
1971	Raza Unida	1,668	1,649	
	Candidates	1,657	1,626	
			1,622	
	Average	1,663	1,632*	31†
	Anti-Raza	1,236	911	
	Unida	1,218	891	
	Candidates		890	
	Average	1,227	897*	330†
1972	Raza Unida	1,727	1,745	
	Candidates	1,707	1,741	
	Average	1,717	1,743	−26
	Anti-Raza	845	517	
	Unida	840	522	
	Candidates			
	Average	843	520	323
1973	Raza Unida	1,661	1,543	
	Candidates	1,657	1,526	
		1,642	1,542	
	Average	1,653	1,537	116

	Anti-Raza	1,223	1,024	
	Unida	1,201	991	
	Candidates	1,205	990	
	Average	1,210	1,002	208
1974	Raza Unida	1,471	1,440	
	Candidates	1,478	1,442	
	Average	1,475	1,441	34
	Anti-Raza	939	779	
	Unida	902	789	
	Candidates			
	Average	921	784	137

* In 1971 three candidates not endorsed by either Raza Unida or the Anti-Raza Unida coalition entered the city council race and received 4, 14, and 40 votes.
† Between the 1970 and 1971 elections, a Mexican American area (Camposanto) was annexed into the city. This small area, which strongly supported Raza Unida, slightly increased the city vote for Raza Unida and slightly decreased the number of Raza Unida votes in the rural areas for the years 1971 and after. The annexation makes the distinction between the Mexican Americans of the city and the county more pronounced, because "Camposanto" was a migrant area. Bearing this point in mind, it makes the 1970 difference between support for Raza Unida in the city and school district (an addition of only 39 votes) even more startling.

essentially two different kinds of landless laborers. The first and most common are the migrant workers. The great majority of these are located inside the city limits of Crystal City. But in the outlying parts of the county, the more common form of landless laborer is not the migrant, but the farm or ranch hand who lives on the land of his Anglo overlord. He is not a tenant, because he does not make autonomous decisions about crops or grazeland, but he is there as a permanent source of labor for the landowner or proprietor. He and his family are provided with housing and in general he has a steady, year-round job. Very few of these Mexican "hands," who are tied to a specific piece of land and to an Anglo boss, migrate.

The contrast between these two types of landless laborers, in terms of availability for political mobilization and radicalization in support of an independent Chicano movement is striking. Both the Anglos and the Raza Unida leadership are aware of these distinctions. But, at a statistical level, it is very hard to measure the difference between the two. This distinction is not made by the United States Bureau of the Census nor by the United States Department of Agriculture. It is thus impossible to determine the actual number of each kind of farm laborer. Bearing in mind, however, that the outlying parts of the county contain few migrants but many farm and ranch hands, a comparison of city and school district electoral data supports the assertion that the political roles of these two kinds of landless laborers are quite distinct.[10]

Table 1 shows the difference in electoral support for Raza Unida candidates in the city and in the school district. The only difference between the two districts is that the school district encompasses, in addition to the city, about half the rural areas of the county, therefore including about one thousand rural people who live outside the city.[11]

The table shows that in every year since La Raza Unida has contested offices for the city government and the school board, they have been victorious by smaller margins in the school district than in the city elections. In percentage points the difference is not large, but when we consider that the only difference between the two districts is the rural area of the school district, which includes only about ten to fifteen percent more people than the city, the results are striking.

Notice, for example, the 1971 elections, which were bitterly fought over the issue of how La Raza Unida had run the government in its first year of rule. The anti-Raza Unida candidates averaged over three hundred more votes in the school district election than in the city election, but the Raza Unida candidates averaged only thirty-one more votes. This indicates that the rural areas were voting overwhelmingly against La Raza Unida, by perhaps a ten-to-one margin or more. Whether the voters were Anglo farmers and ranchers or their Chicano field hands, their votes were anti-Raza Unida.[12]

The rural areas of the school district were not enough to overcome the large city vote in favor of La Raza Unida, but at the countywide level La Raza Unida lost some important elections, and forces for and against the Chicano party were much more equally balanced. County elections not only included the rest of the rural areas of the county not covered in the school district, but two small towns of La Pryor and Batesville as well. Although these two towns were predominantly Mexican-American, they contained fewer migrants and did not have any unionized canneries. La Raza Unida thus found these towns harder to penetrate, although not as inhospitable as the rural areas.

Table 1 also indicates a trend in relative strength. The second most severely fought election after La Raza Unida gained control was in 1973, when control of the two governmental bodies was again at stake. The 1973 results indicated a slight breakthrough in the mammoth rural opposition to the Chicano party. The anti-Raza Unida forces received slightly over two hundred more votes in the school district election than in the city election, but the Raza Unida forces increased their total by over one hundred.[13] This voting seemed to confirm what Raza Unida had suspected—that they were beginning to break the hold of some Anglo landowners and proprietors in a few parts of the county. There was considerable elation, for instance, when the Chicano hands of one of the largest Anglo ranchers in the county reportedly bolted his control and voted for La Raza Unida. This was rare, however, both because Raza Unida faced severe difficulty in reaching these people, and because the farm and ranch hands, being tied to a particular piece of land and dependent upon a particular owner or proprietor, existed in a different social and economic environment from the migrant or cannery worker.

Generalizations on the Role of Migrant Workers

To apply these ideas from the Crystal City experience to all of South Texas, it seems plausible to argue that in general migrants may be considerably more susceptible to political mobilization and radicalization than farm hands who work under a patron. Migrants are not so vulnerable to economic intimidation in their home base area because they earn much of their income elsewhere and because even in their home base they are likely to work for several different employers. Their movement seems to inhibit the development of personal patron-peon relationships. Both these factors seem to free them from strong conservatizing forces. But their geographic mobility and isolation also makes them very hard to reach. The majority of migrants in America are most assuredly outside the political process. To mobilize them requires organizational structure and leadership; but when they are reached, they seem prone to radical politics.

Ozzie Simmons, in his study of Anglo and Mexican-American relations in South Texas years ago, noted even then that differences in types of farm workers made some more vulnerable to control than others. In his study of the Rio Grande Valley, Simmons noted that the *jefes* (political bosses doing the bidding of various Anglo politicians) had as their base those Mexicans who they were able to do favors for. These tended to be permanent residents tied to a particular piece of land which the *jefe* might own. Simmons noted, however, that "by the very nature of the basis of his power, the *jefe* cannot reach the group of field workers in the harvest crews who represent such a large percentage of the total Mexican-American population in the area, nor does he make an attempt to do so."[14] The role of the migrants, and those who worked the farms of many different employers, was thus minimized, Simmons states, because of the lack of contact between the temporary workers and the *jefe,* and the resulting absence of stable relationships with employers who might have provided the stimulus to get them to vote and to vote "right." In Simmons's time the migrants were simply unorganized and outside the political process. Their political activity remained one only of potential.[15]

What Simmons has said about migrants in the Rio Grande Valley relates closely to what Eric Wolf has noted in his more general study of peasant revolts. Wolf has argued that "distinctions of property and involvement in property, in relations to markets, in relations to systems of communication," all seem to be important in understanding and predicting peasant revolts. He has continued that

> the decisive factor in making a peasant rebellion possible lies in the relation of the peasantry to the field of power which surrounds it. A rebellion cannot start from a situation of complete impotence: the powerless are easy victims. . . . The poor peasant or the landless laborer who depends on a landlord for the largest part of his livelihood, or the totality of it, has no tactical power: he is without sufficient resources of his own to serve him as resources in the power struggle. Poor peasants and landless laborers, therefore, are unlikely to pursue the course of rebellion, *unless* they are able to rely on some external power to challenge the power which constrains them.[16]

This generalization fits the Crystal City experience, for Crystal City migrants, by *not* being tied to local landlords, had more political options open to them than those Mexicans who were tied to a particular Anglo employer. And even in Crystal City the "external power" of the Teamsters and the Chicano activists such as Gutiérrez were essential elements in each of the revolts. That is, although the migrants may have been more independent of Anglo political control, an outside catalyst was still needed to provide the organizational skills and manpower to launch a successful challenge to Anglo rule.

The Implications of the Crystal City Mobilization for the Chicano Movement in South Texas

Although further research needs to be undertaken to determine the actual and potential bases of support for the Chicano movement in South Texas, a central thrust of this paper has been that Crystal City could not have experienced either electoral revolt without the migrant workers. The "something more" necessary for successful Chicano mobilization clearly seems in Crystal City to have involved the migrants of the community. For the Chicano movement generally to attempt to base its support primarily upon migrants, however, would not be practical. The right kind of landless laborers are not present in sufficient numbers in other parts of South Texas.[17] Most Mexican Americans are not migrants, and the trend toward mechanization in farming has meant that over the years fewer and fewer jobs are available for migrants. Often underemployed and unemployed, the migrant's place can always be taken by others desperately in search of work, and their services are less important to farmers now than they were prior to the age of mechanization.[18]

Even in Crystal City, as we noted, migrants alone were not enough to cause the revolts. The building of the large Del Monte cannery, and the decision to allow unionization, clearly were important. But if the Chicano movement is to look to unionization as an equally viable base for revolts, the going will be difficult indeed, for unionization is a rare phenomenon in South Texas.[19] The passage of time does not seem to have created a climate any more hospitable for unions. The most serious attempt at unionization in the 1960s was the struggle by the United Farm Workers to organize in the Rio Grande Valley. This ended in failure when Mexico permitted strikebreakers to cross over to work the fields and when the Texas Rangers and local law officials had most of the strike leadership jailed.[20] Unionization, then, cannot yet be a general factor in promoting the mobilization of the Chicano masses.

We have noted the importance of the migrants and the union in the development of the first revolt in Crystal City, and have stressed that in South Texas neither of these factors is common enough to allow one to predict that successful Chicano political revolts will spread. Furthermore, even with the auspicious social and economic requisites that Crystal City did have, we should not forget that the first revolt there failed after two years of governance. This failure leads us to a third factor that seems crucial for the success of the Chicano movement—political leadership.[21] Political leadership must be able to reach and organize these essentially poor and isolated people and relate political phenomena to them in ways they can understand. The second revolt, which was begun by high school students, probably would not have been successful had it not been for the return of Gutiérrez to Crystal City. The kind and quality of leadership in the Chicano movement is very important, and it involves a situation of great delicacy as well. The younger, better-educated, and more radical leadership that are likely to spearhead the movement are separated from the mass of Mexican Americans by their education and by their greater affluence, much as the colonial intellectuals were separated from their native population.[22]

The gap between the leadership and the masses appears essential for other successes in South Texas. At least the history of the first revolt in Crystal City seems to indicate that leadership more truly of the people, truly representative of the Mexican-American population, simply cannot survive in the economic, social, and political structures of South Texas. They will instead be defeated by the legal complexities of government and by the far greater sophistication of the Anglo and middle-class Mexican-American adversaries. Yet as a corollary, for the movement to win more successes, ways must be devised to bridge the gulf between the leadership and masses. In Crystal City this has been done through the creation of a broad-based community organization, which is influential in choosing candidates for office, policies for the governments, and self-help programs. If such ways are not found to bridge the gap, it seems likely that the masses will retreat into apathy or despair, or will be resentful of the "success" of the leadership. And the leadership can always be tempted by inducements the Anglos are able to offer.

Examples of surrounding communities seem to indicate that even in areas where Chicanos are numerically dominant and migrants are an important percentage of the population, the movement can be deflected either through the lack of mass participation and mass mobilization or through inadequacies or cooptation of the leadership. And in areas where Chicanos form a significant portion of the population, but less than half of the voting population, the movement will almost assuredly fail to control governmental structures even if it mobilizes and politicizes the Chicano community.[23]

The foregoing indicates that a militant Chicano takeover of South Texas is unlikely. On the contrary, the results so far indicate that the success story of Crystal City was dependent upon characteristics that have not been at all common to South Texas: not only a homogeneous and largely migrant Mexican-American community lacking "upper-class Spanish" leaders, but an Anglo community accustomed to running the town almost completely on their own; a history of settlement which led to a heavy numerical preponderance of Mexican Americans over Anglos; the presence of an international union; and lastly the development of extremely intelligent, politically astute Mexican leadership. These characteristics which were important in Crystal City are not present in the right combinations in most of South Texas. Where many of the characteristics are present—as in several towns near Crystal City and in the new towns of the Valley —it seems that the lack of any one of them, such as politically astute leadership, can frustrate the entire movement. Crystal City has been an exception, and in the end it is likely to remain an exception—an enclave surrounded by unfriendly forces who control the rest of South Texas.

1. Eric Wolf, *Peasant Wars of the Twentieth Century* (New York, 1963), p. xiv.

2. For the best general history of Mexican-American political activity in the Southwest over the last century, see Alfredo Cuellar, "Perspective on Politics," in Joan Moore, *Mexican Americans* (Englewood Cliffs, N.J., 1970), pp. 137–56.

3. For the best account of economic and labor aspects of this area of South Texas, see Paul Taylor, *An American-Mexican Frontier* (Durham, N.C., 1934).

4. Many of them, in fact, have settled in other parts of the country.

5. For greater detail on the revolts themselves, see my *Chicano Revolt in a Texas Town* (Notre Dame, Indiana, 1974).

6. In using the word *revolt* to describe what has happened in Crystal City, I want to emphasize that it does not here mean the use of violence or the seizing of land and property. The revolts have on the contrary been primarily legal, although they have tried to attack an enormous number of subjects ordinarily not even discussed by South Texas politicians. An interesting question, however, is how much other kinds of revolts, such as nonelectoral ones, may appear in the Chicano movement, and to what extent they may be based on characteristics different from those present in Crystal City.

7. Although I will not dwell upon specific issues and changes brought about by the revolts, I should perhaps note that land reform has been a subliminal issue. Virtually all land in the county is owned by Anglos. The Raza Unida leadership would like to break the hold of the landowners, but thinks it can begin to do so only by greatly increasing property taxes. The school system has aggressively pursued tax increases on this land, but since La Raza Unida (as of 1974) does not have control of the county, county tax-rates have continued much the same.

8. Accurate estimates of the number of migrants anywhere in America are very difficult to find. Two estimates made in the late 1960s, by the Good Neighbor Commission of Texas and the Senate Subcommittee on Migratory Labor, placed the number of migrant workers and their families at between fifty and sixty percent of the total Mexican-American population of the county, ranking it number one in the state. It would be

higher for the city itself, but it would also, of course, vary slightly from year to year depending upon such factors as the availability of local jobs.

9. Another way of attempting to measure migrant worker attitudes—one which hopefully will yield results—would be through sample surveying in the community. This has been attempted rather recently.

10. Census reports reflect this difference. In the rural areas of the Crystal City division, less than one quarter of those families renting homes pay their rent in cash, whereas in the city itself, over ninety percent of those renting homes pay in cash.

    Although not relevant for Crystal City, some farm laborers in the Rio Grande Valley fall in between the two categories mentioned here. That is, they are not migrant laborers, but work several farms in their immediate area, and live not on the land of a patron but in an urban area. Perhaps this group would fall somewhere in the middle in terms of political contrast between the migrants and the hands.

11. Census Bureau divisions do not correspond exactly with the school district, but most of the rural areas of the district are included in the Census Bureau division of Central City. According to the 1970 census estimates approximately sixty-five percent of the people in the rural areas of the Crystal City division said Spanish was their mother tongue. While high, this is somewhat lower than the ratio in the city, which stood at about eighty-five percent. On this basis, one would expect the rural areas of the district to be slightly less receptive to La Raza Unida than the city.

12. I am having to assume here (1) that there was a roughly equal turnout in both districts, and (2) that the same people supporting the Raza Unida slate in the city elections would support them in the school elections (and vice versa). The latter assumption seems to be a fair one, as I found no evidence to the contrary. But figures on the number of eligible voters in each district over the years examined would strengthen our assumption on equal turnout. (In 1972 it seems likely that the turnout was slightly less for the school races than for the city races).

13. Part of the reason that the anti-Raza Unida forces did not gain more votes in the school district may have been because a number of Anglos left the district after the 1971 elections and moved to nearby school districts that were still Anglo-controlled. This exodus would not, however, account for the Raza Unida gain of over one hundred votes, and it is this gain that seems significant.

14. Ozzie Simmons, "Anglo-Americans and Mexican-Americans in South Texas: A Study in Dominant-Subordinate Group Relations," Ph.D. dissertation, Harvard University, 1952, p. 287.

15. To this day the degree of migrant worker participation seems to vary enormously, depending upon whether an organizational structure exists to reach them. It is strong in the Crystal City area, but weaker or nonexistent elsewhere. This fact in part explains why the estimated percentage of migrant workers in a county is not a powerful predictor of support for La Raza Unida. The percentage of migrants does, however, correlate with Raza Unida support far better than does the percentage of Mexican Americans as a whole. A further reason that percentage of migrant workers alone does not predict Raza Unida support more accurately is that Raza Unida support is not limited to migrants. Not only should work be done to determine what other bases of support are possible, but also to see if migrant workers anywhere seem to vote heavily for anti-Chicano movement candidates. If so, they might vote this way through the use of *contratistas.*

16. Wolf, *Peasant Wars,* p. 290.

17. There are signs that the Raza Unida leadership are aware of these dilemmas, and that a number feel the party should devote more energy to mobilizing the Chicanos of larger urban areas or to tempering their cultural ideology so as to appeal to more non-Chicanos. See, for example, Tony Castro, "La Raza Unida Leadership Changes Emphasis," *Race Relations Reporter,* Oct. 7, 1974, pp. 1–2.

18. Permanently employed farm and ranch hands are also less common now. Mechanization has affected these landless laborers as well, and many farmers would prefer not to bother with housing and benefits, such as social security, that federal laws now say they must provide. Increasingly, Mexican Americans have had to seek work in other sectors of the economy than agriculture.

19. The Teamsters' experience in the first Crystal City revolt hardly encouraged them to try to develop political power elsewhere in South Texas. The Teamsters were badly burned, and in the years that followed, they gradually turned into a company union. In 1973 they abandoned Crystal City altogether, and a Chicano union now is recognized at the plant.

20. Some might consider the results of the Farah strike in El Paso a good omen, but that struggle lasted two years, and would not have been successful without the backing of a national union and a national boycott. Even then, the actual settlement was a disappointment to the strikers, and several of Farah's plants are likely to remain closed.

21. Some observers have been tempted to say that leadership is virtually the only criterion of any importance—that a leader as charismatic and clever as Gutiérrez could have brought about a similar revolt in virtually any South Texas community that was heavily Mexican American.

As the reasoning in this paper hopefully makes clear, I disagree with this view.

22. This phenomenon of having Raza Unida leadership based on the most educated and acculturated members of the Mexican community—those who understand the system best—has produced a number of ironies. One of the greatest is that this leadership has itself been far more Anglicized than many of the Mexicans who have been supporters of the Anglos. It has also produced the irony of many Chicanos arguing for their rights as American rather than Mexican citizens. For a definite segment of the Mexican-American population, their view of themselves as Americans seems itself to have been a radicalizing influence. In noting this, one Raza Unida leader has commented that the Mexican Americans of the border communities are often more conservative in part because they still compare themselves with Mexicans of Mexico. This comparison, he has argued, leads them to feel gratified that they are better off than the Mexicans on the other side of the river rather than to feel angry that they are not as well off as the Anglos.

23. The question of "failure" and "success" of Chicano revolts hinges in part upon my definition of Chicano revolt. As we noted earlier, other kinds of Chicano revolts are possible besides electoral ones. Even in the electoral arena, it is possible that something less than a revolt of the magnitude of Crystal City's might be possible in circumstances where conditions are not quite so favorable. That is, a coalition of Mexicans and Blacks, or of Mexicans, Blacks, Labor, and Anglo liberals might be possible that could implement some of the changes that have occurred in Crystal City. In fact, in a few places in South Texas Anglos have attempted to undercut the possibility of revolts by introducing a few reforms and working to strengthen "responsible" Mexican-American elements in their areas. Thus, in focusing upon the dramatic political confrontation in Crystal City, one may ignore more subtle ways in which Chicanos may eventually gain influence and power in other parts of South Texas.

Rural Collective Action and the State: A Discussion

RICHARD NEWBOLD ADAMS*

IRRESPECTIVE OF WHAT MAY HAVE BEEN THE ORGANIZERS' IN-
tent, the subject of these papers is rural collective action. Although
assigned the topic of "Comparative Peasant Movements," each author has moved in the direction that his own materials permitted.
Peasants figure large in most of them, but are in no way the only
population of concern, and are even inconsequential in Shockley's
paper. Tilly provides a vast scope, Europe over five hundred years,
and necessarily looks to common factors among many cases; Broomfield looks to the interior social relations of a single Indian state and
finds inherent in them "conservative forces" that inhibit any movement toward widespread rural reform; Katz compares three movements during the Mexican Revolution, and finds that the real control
of events always remained with whomever dominated the central
government; that provincial people were provincial, and unprepared
to take the reins of national destiny; Saul focuses on the contemporary problem of rural mobilization for a socialist society in Africa,
and the problems that confront it; and Shockley concludes with
limits on revolt and social change that are open to Chicanos of the
southwestern United States.

To seek a common theme among all papers is necessarily to focus
on variables that have not necessarily been central to each author's
own interests; but just as they found their way by seeking order in
their data, so I will go where these materials seem to lead me. All
papers clearly see their peasant and rural activities as derived in some
manner from capitalism; less explicit in most, but equally evident, is

*I am indebted to Charles Tilly and John Shockley for comments on an earlier draft of this
paper.

the role of government and the state. The general theme that I will pursue is that the dominant set of variables that generate and terminate rural collective actions will be traced to the state.

Tilly's framework provides the major dynamics of much that follows later. The development of capitalism, that is, commercialism, urbanization, and industrialization, and of what he calls "statemaking," are the major elements contributing to the decline of the peasant. The role of capitalism is recognized in all the remaining papers, how expansive commercial and industrial processes shape and determine the parameters of life in the countryside, and certainly is consonant with the general findings of Eric J. Hobsbawm (1959) and Eric Wolf (1969).

Interplaying with capitalism is the theme of the concentration of power in the state, the construction of the nation. Here again Tilly sets the central theme, and it finds similar elements in the competition among the various segments and quasi-groups of Bengal for political power; the ultimate domination of Villa and Zapata by Carranza in Mexico, and the government manipulation in continuing control of the rural peoples; Tanzania's effort to bring about a rural revolution *in situ* against the "middle peasants" and emerging farmers and proletariat; the problems of mobilization by a counter-state in Mozambique; and the competition of labor unions, political parties, and the U.S. government for the allegiance of the Chicano in South Texas.

Historic capitalism and consolidation of the nation state are clearly grand themes of our times. Yet it is not easy to disentangle their interplay, to identify one or the other as being clearly the more responsible for the events under consideration. Some argue that the two are comesurable. Wallerstein holds that "The distinctive feature of a capitalist world-economy is that economic decisions are oriented primarily to the arena of the world-economy, while political decisions are oriented primarily to the smaller structures that have legal control, the states (national-states, city-states, empires) within the world-economy" (1974, 67).

This also implies that there is a kind of equivalence and differentiation between the decisions made in the capitalist world-economic system on the one hand, and of those of a state on the other hand;

151

this, it seems to me, is untenable. Capitalism is the accumulation of many elements that emerged separately. The most recent elements began with the expanding city-state commercialism of the thirteenth and fourteenth centuries, and the territorial state mercantilism of the sixteenth and seventeenth centuries, and finally the industrialism of the eighteenth, nineteenth, and twentieth centuries. Today capitalism is the world's most important control system, a way of manipulating the energy and material flow of societies. It does this through the use of money, market places, the reckoning of market values, credit mechanisms, organizational devices such as the joint stock company, the notions of reinvestment and the corporation, the fostering of science and engineering, an ideology of expansion, and through the rampant exploitation of human and other natural resources.

Seeing capitalism in this manner requires that we also see it as forming part of the culture and environment of human groups. The kinds of groups that find themselves dealing with at least some of these elements range from fairly primitive chiefdoms to the emergent international blocs. Although the papers under discussion here are concerned with nation-states, Africa illustrates the role of capitalism in societies of a less complex kind, and the history of western colonialism includes many others. If capitalism is a complex of of devices, then the actors that use these devices are individual human beings, and among the most important of whom are those who are trying to make nations. Few decisions can really be made in the "arena of the world-economy" that do not also weigh as political decisions of concern to statemakers. While it is popular to speak of "world capitalism" as if it were an articulated network against which human groups compete, in fact it is a monster with no central nervous system. Rather, it is a technology, a body of knowledge, an assemblage of equipment, an existing series of controls; and it has to do with the physical world of natural resources, men, products, distance, and time. Capitalism, as such, makes no decisions in favor of its own survival; only human groups, nations, chiefdoms, bands, and kingdoms can do this. Among the human groups that make decisions, those that understand capitalism better use it more effectively; those that understand it less tend to lose.

152

Capitalism, however, is by no means the only weapon available to the statemakers, and it can be used by decision makers at their convenience. In the early period of European commercialism this was clear when Charles VII of France stripped Jacques Coeur of his financial empire; when Carlos V and Felipe II declared repeated bankruptcies, thereby destroying one set of banking houses after another; when Elizabeth I of England issued state monopolies; or when Isabel of Castile rejected the offer of the Duke of Mendinaceli for three ships for Columbus, remarking that "Kingdoms of such immense grandure are not to be made without kings!" (Beneyto, 1961, pp. 194–95) More recently state socialism came into being by explicitly removing capitalist devices from the hands of individual citizens, and concentrating them in the hands of the state, to be used not for the individual welfare of private persons, but for the general welfare of the larger population of the society. Socialist states have not given up capitalism; they have merely made it a government monopoly. In their dealings with other states, they must still go to the market place.

Peasants apparently come into being with early capitalism and go out with its full development, and they seem to do this in the context of statemaking. Tilly's 500-year framework gives us an important perspective on this, but it is not quite ample enough. Both the state and capitalism have precursors that had similar interplay, and other groups found themselves marginalized or subordinated by virtue of that action.

The peasant antecedents have to be sought in man's early political economic relations. For this we need to begin with societies that are simpler than those dealt with (except marginally by Saul in Africa) in the present set of papers. Let us conceive of the evolution of human societies schematically to have consisted of a series of stages of increasing numbers of power and levels of integration: bands, chiefdoms, kingdoms, nations, and blocs. (The rationale for this will be found in Adams, 1975.) Higher level societies have acquired greater control over the environment, thereby enabling them to remain more sedentary, and become occupied in more complex industries and specialities. In achieving a higher level, a society becomes more complex, incorporates lesser units in new subordinate capaci-

153

ties, and promotes a new centralizing relations that gives the society as a whole unity within the now larger realm (see Figure 1).

OPERATIONAL LEVEL OF INTEGRATION	MAXIMUM LEVEL OF SOCIETY IN QUESTION				
	BAND	CHIEFDOM	KINGDOM	NATION	BLOC
BLOC					
NATION				India 1970 Mexico 1970	USA 1970 Europe 1970
KINGDOM			Tanzania 1974 Mozambique 1974	Mexico 1910 Europe 1500 Mozambique 1970	
CHIEFDOM					
BAND					Crystal City

FIGURE 1. Evolutionary Framework of Cases Discussed

Within this framework, we are interested in certain aspects of two major processes, the control over goods and power over men. The control over goods, specifically with reference to distribution, has always been of central concern to many. From one standpoint, it may be argued that the decisions over distribution have always been constricted by the definition of the social relations involved. Some relations called for sharing, others called for some kind of equivalency of exchange, and yet others called for getting what you could with no regard for the subsequent relationships (cf. Sahlins, 1972, Chapter 5). Some students of the evolution of economics have held that relations of the last type did not mark early man, but that they have become overwhelming, especially under capitalism (Polanyi *et al.*, 1957). I prefer to argue that in all societies there is a concern for both "giving" and for "taking," but that the former takes precedence in those relations where the contacts are of a continuing person-to-person variety, and are defined as being "within" the group; and that the concern for "taking" predominates in relations that hold between peoples of different groups.

What has been called the market in economics is a very complex matter, but clearly one aspect of it is that those who participate in it are more concerned with taking than with giving; both buyer and seller participate principally in order to get something, goods, money, etc., and giving is a means. The giving and taking differentiates conduct within a group from that outside it early in human evolution.* But taking has many facets among which it is not always possible to differentiate forms except by the definition given from a particular viewpoint. Henri Pirenne observed that "The Vikings, in fact, were pirates, and piracy is the first stage of commerce. So true is this that when their raids ceased, they simply became merchants" (quoted in Dillard, 1967, p. 17). The activities of the Spanish, Dutch, and English in the early colonizing period involved plunder, since it was the only sure way of recovering one's capital investment. Indeed, it is argued that early capitalist industries were specifically oriented toward distant markets, markets where the producer did not have to directly deal with the ultimate consumer; the laborer thereby knew nothing of the market where his labor was being "sold." The continuum of how to treat strangers includes war and the market, and the capitalist system is merely one, although perhaps the most sophisticated and complex, of a series of interrelated devices to handle exchange in this situation.

Obviously, the intergroup relational dimension was not invented with the market or with capitalism. What has happened is that as societies expanded and became more complex, the circle within which giving was of principle concern remained essentially the same in absolute size, i.e., that of a primitive band at the maximum, with an immediate operating component on the order of thirty people, and a maximum group of "known" people on the order of five hundred. As power increased in the system, levels piled up on levels, the dominant concern in exchange relations between minimal relation system inevitably took on the character of a kind of war, specifically the market. No large-scale social order could emerge and survive for any period based on internal piracy and plunder; the formation of larger social units could not take place without being able to "take,"

*Which determined which is probably a meaningless question; that is, whether the question to whom one gave determined who was on the inside, or who was on the inside determined to whom one gave, was to speak of two aspects of a single event; one did not determine the other except from the point of view of an observer. Whether the color of an elephant determines that it is an elephant, or that it is an elephant determines its color, is a meaningless question, except from the point of view of an observer who has only limited access to evidence. If a man saw only a flash of color, he may determine from that that is was an elephant; if he is asked how to get some gray hide, he may decide that he can do that by getting an elephant.

but to do so in a peaceful way. The marketplace and the market (i.e., exchange) notion of value were inventions that made this possible. With the market, larger organizations did not need to be torn apart internally simply because they were too big for small-scale giving relations. But the fact that these market inventions removed the violence from taking did not change the fact that to take implied a loss for someone; the market merely allowed larger organizations to exist. Combined with the right proportion of violence, the market also permitted one society or state to gain at the expense of another. Thus western European expansion was the expansion of states, using first the antecedents of, then capitalism itself, as an important adjunct to war.

In the course of evolution, the "taking" relations that existed between autonomous units, sovereign societies at any level—whether the band, chiefdom, kingdom, or nation—were antecedents of capitalism. Similarly "taking" relations held between competitors for internal control in those societies, whether between individuals or organized groups. Efforts to institute a broad human socialism could achieve some success within such a unit, but could not be established between them. Whether a given society succeeds in achieving socialism internally is a question of immediate resources, strategy, and tactics; to achieve it between societies, however, would require a reversal of a cardinal characteristic of evolution. To see how the market, commercialism, and capitalism relates to the question of the peasant, we must now return to the question of the emergence of the state.

Chiefdoms, familiar to us in terms of the Hawaiian society at the time of contact, or among many of the African tribes that were brought under colonial rule in the last century, were based on various kinds of agricultural (or other high yielding neotechnic technologies) production units that were also residential- and kin-organized. These cultivators were the forerunners of peasants, and, strictly speaking, conform to Tilly's characterization. In recent years, however, the term peasant has tended to be used, and is so used by all our participants, to refer not to these chiefdom level tillers, but to their corresponding types that evolved within the development of the state. This happened first in what we are calling kingdoms, societal organizations of the kind that were centralizing territorial power in the thirteenth and fourteenth centuries in Europe, were present in South and West Africa in the nineteenth century, but had surely appeared frequently in the previous centuries. The regional dominions of pre-British India included kingdoms, but in many areas the effective level of society was still that of the chiefdom. The Moguls, Broomfield notes, "had incorporated most parts of north and central India under one rule," but, "large areas of Bengal had remained in independent principalities."

For practical purposes we may distinguish chiefdoms from kingdoms by the fact that the former relied to a great extent on the allocation of power by subchiefs, subordinate leaders who have the immediate allegiance of a following; and the acceptance of a common religious system. In kingdoms, the subchiefs have been subordinated to the king, the elemental bureaucracies have taken over critical functions of decision making, and religion is supplemented to a critical degree by military force. The nation, in turn, displaces religion as a societal unifier entirely, with various secular ideologies, depends on a high degree of military (including police) force for public order, and is based on an industrial system, either its own, or through dependence on those of other nations.

In the course of these expansions in scale, the cultivator of the chiefdom becomes increasingly subordinated. "Kings" may resort to a kind of royal populism to assure themselves of power, but the peasant is fundamentally in a continuing state of tension with the demands of tribute, taxes, and markets; and his welfare and opportunities answer principally to the relative population density. Where the population is scarce and resources ample, the peasant enjoys his classical autonomy; but as peasants become numerous, and as resources become restricted, then he falls prey to the competition of the nobles or capitalists who usually increasingly force him into a dependency status as serf, slave, sharecropper, client, or proletarian. This is the classic peasant, answerable in tribute to a king or noble, and subjected to the irregular use of capitalist expansion and displacement.

To return to our cases, it is clear that the state is the critical actor in the later phases of evolution in Europe and the New World. In

Africa, however, the extension of kingdoms over large areas were not native, but the imperial extensions, of first, expanding European kingdoms, and later with the increased use of capitalist elements derived from industrialism in Europe, the extension of imperial nations. This led to the subverting of chiefdoms where cultivators had not been subject to classical peasant status previously. Saul makes clear how Tilly's argument that capitalism destroys peasants is paradoxically reversed, for it is the capitalistic colonial expansion that creates peasants from chiefdom and tribal cultivators who were not subject to state system before. But the African peasant emergence is recent, and as a result peasantization and proletarianization are going on simultaneously. Saul quotes Colin Leys' observation that the "peasantry in Africa may be best seen as a transitional class, in between the period of primitive cultivators living in independent communities and that of capitalist development in which peasants are restratified into capitalists and proletarians . . ."

The issues that really concern Saul are less the structural questions themselves and more the tactical consequences of how such a peasantry is to be politicized and collectivized. He observes that efforts by an "external vanguard," a counter-state, generally had greater initial success in the more proletarianized regions, but he resists being "categoric in these matters." Efforts to push active participation in a revolution, notes Saul, will not work with peasants if the "leadership does not appear to present a genuine and less exploitative alternative than does the colonial system itself. They thus exercise a kind of passive veto over the movement and those who lead it." There is no question that the liberation forces in Portuguese Africa are politically more sophisticated than was Zapata; but they are not local people, and must cover great sectors of a continent, widely differentiated tribal, proletarian, and peasant populations, and until recently, a clear-cut colonial military regime of unquestioned intent.

Tanzania, the other portion of the great continent on which Saul reports, brings us back from the extreme of active peasant revolution to a situation much more akin in many respects to Bengal; or, better said, to one that seems to be marching in the direction of Bengal. Independence offered an apparent opportunity to create a somewhat socialist state, especially within the peasantry. The train of events has, however, led increasingly toward local capitalism, the increasing emergence of middle-level peasants, of "kulaks." The efforts of Nyerere from the state level to establish local socialism have been encountering severe difficulties. They stem from the fact that to build a state structure the government must rely heavily on the domestic unit agriculturalists and cottage industries for both popular and economic support. For Nyerere to impose the kind of economic processes involved in socialism, his government must be much stronger than it currently is. It is not yet clear whether the FRELIMO of Mozambique can convert peoples who have received their status under the pressure of capitalism if there is not some statelike power source to sustain them. Certainly some of the workers in the movement recognized the dangers, as evidenced by remarks suggesting that the very existence of Portuguese opposition was important in gaining the strength necessary. Now that Portuguese pressure is relaxed, and the liberation movements must continue with neither the advantage of an enemy nor yet that of a strong state, it is likely that the Portuguese ex-colonies will encounter problems similar to those of Tanzania.

In Bengal what were probably chiefdoms were brought under an extended period of colonial rule. An important relational system emergent in societies at the chiefdom level is the patron-client, or clientage, relation. A major interest of British colonialism was to extract raw materials and exploit new markets both within India and elsewhere. To do this, it coopted the existing Indian political system. This essentially meant that while the demands of the British were met at the highest levels, a basic Indian system continued to evolve at all the lower levels. The complexity of the Bengal scene, as so penetratingly described by Broomfield, is that of a society that has evolved in place, carrying with it the readaptation of patron-client dependency patterns, now extended and active at all levels. In this situation, the peasants are only one of a number of socioeconomic types involved in crosscutting competitions that tend to neutralize serious efforts by the nation-state to extend power over its extraordinarily diverse and widespread peoples.

But the process of statemaking has never been one where the peasants *become* the state; in Bengal, as in Europe before it, the state is evolving by the expanding successful dominance of the middle levels. "Why no peasant revolution?" asked Broomfield. "The answer clearly is that the conservative forces in the countryside had not been weakened in these years. Moreover, it was their political organizations, based in the rural towns, which were now devoted to communal confrontation." Statemaking occurs by the identification of common interests by a centralizing organism and not only its immediate sources of support, its retainers, but also the lesser power holders, the regional leaders and bosses, landowners, traders, or what you will. As against this combination, the more marginalized sectors of the society grow in numbers, but not in wealth. The socialist alternative of trying to identify the centralizing organism with the more numerous marginalized sectors, displacing the immediate and regional retainers, can work only if there is a way to organize the former. The classic Marxist answer was to turn to the urbanized proletariat; but Wolf (1969) has argued, and some of these papers sustain him, that the peasant community can also play this role if it has some organizational base. What Broomfield describes are conditions of peasant communities that have been fragmented through caste and religious factionalism, and through interlocking networks of clientage. Moreover, the leadership of these communities lies not with a passionate and self-sacrificing Zapata, but rather in the hands of the mobility-ready, self-seeking, local and provincial, middle class, who themselves comprise a system that is always beckoning to the ambitious newcomer. Like the slot machine, it lets only a very few win. Thus the multipatroned system always has newly aggressive and climbing elements to sustain it; it cannot grow old, it cannot mature, nor can it become rotten enough to fall victim to a revolt. Although idealistic African politicians may look to China as a model of the future, Bengal may lie closer to the truth.

Mexico parallels the Bengal case in a very general way, but differs in two important historical particulars. First, it shifted from a direct colonial dependency a century and a quarter before India did; and second, it suffered a crippling population loss in the colonial period, and the nineteenth century saw the regrowth of this population. Thus, Mexico also experienced a recent chiefdom condition, but it was really due first to colonial depopulation, then reduction of effective rule to local and regional caciques and caudillos with the end of the Spanish Empire. The latter half of the nineteenth century saw the expansion of agrarian capitalism and urban industrialism in Mexico, and with it, the attack on the peasantry that paralleled the European experience in many respects. In Mexico, too, strong patron-client relations evolved, and these marked not only the revolutionary period but continue today to be characteristic of much of Latin America. What has been taking place in Mexico, and is also suggested for India, is that the individual patron is being displaced; the landlord, the cacique, the caudillo, the ambitious politician is replaced by the government and its manifold agents. Today, in a nation of pristine (though polluted) capitalism, the government of the nation is the major dispenser of goods and benefits. In 1910, however, the government was not widely dispensing such benefits and at that time the rapidly growing peasant population was being divested of its land by an even more rapidly growing agrarian capitalism. The haciendas of Morelos had expanded within a few generations. For the peasant it was not a slow attrition, but a rapid rape. Both the speed of the loss and the unavailability of open and alternative lands within the region forced the peasants to be acutely aware of their losses. Unlike small holders caught in the web of clientage, they had nothing to offer but their labor, and hence were worthless as clients. But they did have strong communities, not yet shattered by capitalist penetration. Kindred in frustration, as well as in language, religion, blood, and marriage, the peasants of Morelos offered a reasonably good approximation to the ideal peasant population for organization. The critical question, given the appropriate conditions, was leadership.

The appearance of peasant leaders is not unlike the appearance of genetic mutants. Mutation is going on constantly, but most are lethal; they are self-destructive and do not reproduce. The few that do survive the always threatening environment are subject to genetic drift, that is, they may be easily eliminated by "accidents." Thus the appearance of a peasant leader is itself not uncommon; what is uncommon is he survives with personal goals identified with the welfare of his clients, and not be subverted by middle-level patrons. Certainly Mexico was similar to Bengal in the growing patron-client system; it was simply that the dispossessed Morelos peasants were too poor, and too recently poor, to be clients. But they had been peasants and they were acutely ready for a reactive movement (in Tilly's sense of the term).

The Mexican Revolution had a further consequence in Texas. Many Mexicans came north, some driven from their communities and their land, others simply to escape the devestation of the Revolution. There began the movement of Mexican labor to the United States, labor from a peasant population that was to grow in a country with insufficient available land for peasants, and a state dedicated to using the capitalist implement in pursuit of its own development. North of the border, U.S. farmers found in this a new source of extremely cheap labor; an almost ideal "reserve army" of migrants who could be present when needed, but who would melt away when the wages stopped because they had to survive and, with no state protection, had to seek other economic alternatives. "All Crystal City was ever intended to be," noted a Shockley informant, "was a labor camp!"

The United States, if we look again to Figure 1, has to be seen in the 'Bloc' column. The United States is a nation, but not just any capitalist nation, it is *the* capitalist nation that took the mantle from Great Britain in the early twentieth century. Its dedication to "nationmaking" has, since the World War II, been somewhat subordinated to "blocmaking," and the appearance of a continuing circulation of Mexican laborers in its southwestern lands is more a matter of interest to local politicians and landowners, than to the nation. In the 1960s, along with various ethnic political movements, the resident population of Mexican extraction (for that is the commonality; many have come only recently, but some can claim ancestry to the Spanish population of the colonial era) became one of the less militant, but a visibly marginal populations. State governments, closely allied with local wealth (the governor of Texas at the time of writing was also the state's greatest landholder and a long time employer of illegal Mexican migrant labor) were generally unwilling to answer these challenges; the federal government, however, seeking votes from across the nation, could afford to provide some such help. Moreover, Anglo-American labor was angry at what low-wage earning migrants were able to accomplish in the labor market. So first the

Teamster Union, then the U.S. Government, supplied help of one kind or another to the Crystal City Chicano effort to organize and confront the local Anglo population.

John Shockley's report on the role of migrants in the political revolts at Crystal City, Texas, underscores Tilly's conclusion that capitalism has little use for peasants; it further underscores Marx's original classic argument (taken to task in Saul's paper) that proletarians are the most likely people to be significant in such actions. The Chicano case is hardly critical insofar as the argument over the mobilizable qualities of peasants versus proletarians, but it does suggest that small farms, not to speak of subsistence farmers, have had a hard time against the expansion of great agro-businesses, and that what peasants there may be (in the Tilly sense) are few. The burden of Shockley's argument is that the Crystal City migrants working in the vegetable fields, together with unionized chicanos in the local cannery, formed the backbone of support for the electoral rebellions that have now occurred twice within a decade. He sustains this by comparing voting data from presumed chicanos who were (to use Katz's term) *acasillados,* resident in outlying ranches and within the district and the county limits. The intimidation of the farm employee by his boss makes it difficult for him to rise to the level of political action.

Let us now turn to Tilly's classification of collective action. The first, the *competitive,* he finds in the literature on peasants, and it must be recognized that under his definition of "collective action," there are such movements. But for present purposes, Tilly's *competitive* movements are of quite a different order than either the *reactive* and the *proactive.* They are not peculiar to peasants, but are found among the roughly equivalent units of any society. The reactive and proactive movements, however, emerge in the structure of dominance, and therefore are more importance in the present context. Placing these two types of movements in the context of Figure 1 indicates that the reactive movements are typical of the kingdom phase; the proactive movements are typical of the national phase: and this, I believe, is congruent with what Tilly was arguing. What may not be as evident, however, is that the proactive movements are more than merely attempts to create rights within the larger context of the nation; they are also competitive, although they differ from the earlier competitive movements of Tilly in that the perpetrators may not know with whom it is they may be competing. They are, of course, competing with whomever is currently benefiting from what they want; and this, as often as not, is the capitalist, the governmental bureaucrat, or the many that live their lives in the protected domain of these actors.

Proaction and reaction have something of the quality of Weberean ideal types. They can also easily become projections that conform to the interests of those who see them. In Latin America today many movements of peasants, laborers, and others of the lower sector have been called "revindicative," implying that whatever it is that is being sought originally pertained to those who now seek it. By the same token, those who are now in control, the leaders and powerful sectors, do not see these movements as revindicative. If they were forced into Tillian terminology, they would argue that the movements are proactive, that things are being sought that never were available before. No doubt in given cases, historical research would reveal to what degree each of the viewpoints may be valid; but such research is unlikely since the issues are those of praxis, of survival, not of academic classification.

If we attempt to place the various cases from Mexico, Bengal, Mozambique, Tanzania, and Crystal City in the Tillian classification, there are some problems. The Mexican cases illustrate the issues. Zapata's revolt would presumably be classifiable as reactive. It comprised peasants who recently lost their land, and who mobilized to regain it. Crystal City would equally appear to be proactive. Although democratic processes and majority rule were in some manner "guaranteed" them in the United States law, the migrants and Chicanos had, in fact, never enjoyed those rights. So while they sought what was rightfully theirs, the movement has to be considered as proactive since it sought something they never had. The Villa movement, and that reported from Yucatán, however, seem to fit neither of the categories. The northern Mexican movement was an unbelievable combination of hacendados, politicians, small farmers, ranch hands, cowboys, peasants, and urban laborers—a fruit salad that found its anger and unity in the fact that it was not the main course.

Unlike the Zapatistas who wanted only their land, the *Norteños* were a regional mixed society that rose to get their share of the goodies in the larger system. Bolstered by funds and arms from U.S. interests, and ultimately re-establishing the same fundamental system that they had presumably risen against, it is difficult to see them as a peasant movement. They sought what they did not have, and so were proactive; but they sought it under a reactive ideology and were paradoxically seen by many outsiders to be parallel in their structure to the Morelos peasants.

The Yucatán case is even more difficult. It began as an organized government action repressing an existing conservative revolt of *hacendados*. In order for the government to retain its dominance, Alvarado resorted to populist devices. He established a massive clientage system where he gave higher wages and ended debt peonage. Shall we say that the laborers were coopted into a reactive movement relieving them of indenture, and a proactive one for higher wages?

The problem is clearly not that some of these cases deal with peasants and some do not. Tilly's classification deals explicitly with "rural collective action," action by people whose predominent total community time is devoted to agricultural production. Rather, the problem lies in how to relate the dynamic conditions that produced collective action with a typology of collective action.

Let us return to capitalism and statemaking. Statemaking is essentially replicative; that is, at each level of human social evolution, there is some kind of centralization of power; this is the "making" process in "statemaking," "nationmaking" or "blocmaking." At the higher levels, this has been called the "state," but that is clearly a folk usage with little analytical utility. Unlike statemaking, capitalism is a conjunction and interrelation of a series of distinctive cultural traits that in one combination or another provide an economic mechanism for greater concentration of control over energetic forms. Thus capitalism is something "new" in history; statemaking is the replication of a pattern of concentration of power.

Is it the case, as was suggested earlier, that reactive movements are peculiar to the kingdom phase of evolution? Certainly in European history, rural peoples found the losses to the combined activities of the state and capitalism to be insufferable, and resorted to move-

165

ments that were, by definition, reactive. But obviously reactions to losses can occur under many other circumstances and for many other purposes. The interesting thing about Tilly's analysis is that he sees the end of European rural reactive movements to have been due on the one hand to the increased power of the state to simply repress such action, and on the other, to the disappearance of local organizational forms on which such collective action could be based. This last, in turn, was due at least in part to the transformational effect of capitalism on the countryside. In a sense, capitalism and the state together are the despoilers that bring on a reactive movement that the state then must confront in order to re-establish the order of a new system. Reactive movements were, thus, anti-statemaking.

Proactive movements, as described by Tilly for Europe, are more complex in their structure, for now the peasants are undergoing proletarianization, and the proactive movements tend to be a "combination of a nucleus of skilled but threatened workers with a larger mass of unskilled workers in closely related employment . . ." Proactions, says Tilly, "contended over national policies, national markets and national structure of power to a degree unheard of in the earlier reactive waves of collective action." Thus proactive movements imply an actual competition over who is going to enjoy power within the expanding state, who is going to determine the nature of the state being made. If this is the case, then we can more readily see the Villa movement as being proactive. Moreover, we can also see movements in Bengal and that of the resistance to government village programs in Tanzania and the insurgent military developments in Mozambique, to be competing for determining the shape of the future and, as such, proactive.

The Tilly classification, then, is suggestive of another set of definitions. Reactive movements are anti-statemaking; that is, they are movements directed at retaining a decentralization of power, of inhibiting the concentration of power that capitalism provides for capitalists and for the state. Proactive movements are not against statemaking but are attempts to get in on the available benefits, in on the decision making as to how the state and economy shall be run. In this sense, the Yucatán events described by Katz would be a government proactive answer to a proactive movement on the part of the hacendados.

To oversimplify, kingdoms took the cultivators of the chiefdoms, and with the help of capitalistic antecedents, converted them into peasants. Peasants have a place in kingdoms. But as industrial nations emerged, peasants were found to have no place, so capitalism was then used as an implement to help eradicate them. Thus the variable is in the nature of the statemaking, and not in the capitalism. Russia found the kulaks no more convenient than Nyerere finds the peasant villages. Peasants ideally reject full integration into any state system; they will pay it only what they are forced to, and will contribute to the market only what is absolutely necessary for their own exchange needs. Their focus is on the household and kin-community, both as an economic unit and a domain of authority. But like any political-economic type, peasants have their specific locus in history and evolution. They have a place in kingdoms, but not in nations, whether socialistic or capitalistic.

REFERENCES

Adams, Richard Newbold
1975 *Energy and Structure: A Theory of Social Power.* Austin: University of Texas Press.

Dillard, Dudley
1967 *Economic Development of the North Atlantic Community.* Englewood Cliffs, New Jersey: Prentice Hall, Inc.

Hobsbawm, Eric
1965 *Primitive Rebels.* New York: W.W. Norton and Company.

Polanyi, Karl, Arensberg, Conrad M.; and Pearson, Harry W., eds.
1957 *Trade and Markets in the Early Empires.* Glencoe: The Free Press and the Falcon's Wing Press.

Sahlins, Marshall
1972 *Stone Age Economics.* Chicago and New York: Aldine-Atherton, Inc.

Wallerstein, Immanuel
1974 *The Modern World-System. Capitalist Agriculture and the Origins of the European World Economy in the Sixteenth Century.* New York: Academic Press.

Wolf, Eric R.
1969 *Peasant Wars of the Twentieth Century.* New York, etc.: Harper and Row.